eXplore

Bible notes for adults

January – March 2011

In this issue

The 90 daily readings in this issue of *Explore* are designed to help you understand and apply the Bible as you read it daily. Sections in this edition include readings from Genesis, Philippians, 1 Chronicles, John and the psalms.

It's serious!

We suggest that you allow 15 minutes each day to work through the Bible passage with the notes. It should be a meal, not a snack! Readings from other parts of the Bible can throw valuable light on the study passage. These cross-references can be skipped if you are already feeling full up, but will expand your grasp of the Bible.

Sometimes a prayer box will encourage you to stop and pray through the lessons—but it is always important to allow time to pray for God's Spirit to bring His word to life, and to shape the way we think and live through it.

We're serious!

All of us who work on *Explore* share a passion for getting the Bible into people's lives. We fiercely hold to the Bible as God's word—to honour and follow, not to explain away.

Contributors to this issue

- Christopher Ash • Tim Chester •
- John Richardson •
- Tim Thornborough • Anne Woodcock •

For information on how to subscribe, and our other Bible-teaching and training materials, please visit:

UK & Europe: www.thegoodbook.co.uk
N America: www.thegoodbook.com
Australia: www.thegoodbook.com.au
New Zealand: www.thegoodbook.co.nz

or contact us at admin@thegoodbook.co.uk

How to use Explore

Find a time you can read the Bible each day

Find a place where you can be quiet and think

Ask God to help you understand

Carefully read through the Bible passage for today

Study the verses with *Explore*, taking time to think

Pray about what you have read

Welcome to Explore—a resource to help you dig into, understand and apply the timeless truth of God's word to your life.

It can be a struggle to find a daily time to spend with God. Children, the busyness of life, special nights out, holidays, or just sheer exhaustion can all conspire to get in the way. However, there is no substitute for just getting into a good habit. There are many patterns that suit different people, and yours may change over time.

Whatever you choose to do, guard your time with God jealously. If you come hungry to learn from the Lord, and to feed on the truth, it will be a place of nurture and growth, and a source of direction and strength for your daily life.

TIME: Find a time when you will not be disturbed, and when the cobwebs are cleared from your mind. Many people have found that the morning is the best time, as it sets you up for the day. You may not be a 'morning person' so last thing at night, or, if you're free, a mid-morning break suits others. Whatever works for you is right for you.

PLACE: Jesus says that we are not to make a great show of our religion (see Matthew 6 v 5-6), but rather pray with the door to our room shut. So, anywhere you can be quiet and private is the key. Some people plan to get to work a few minutes earlier and get their Bible out in an office, or some other quiet corner.

PRAYER: Although *Explore* helps with specific prayer ideas from the passage, you should try to develop your own lists to pray through. Use the flap inside the back cover to help with this.

Often our problem is not so much *who* to pray for, as *what to pray for them*! That's why Bible reading and prayer are inseparable. We are reminded from God's word of what is truly important; it will shape what we pray for ourselves, the world and others.

SHARE: As the saying goes: *expression deepens impression*. So try to cultivate the habit of sharing with others what you have learned. It will encourage both them and you. Using the same notes as a friend will help you encourage each other to keep going.

REMEMBER:

- **IT'S QUALITY, NOT QUANTITY, THAT COUNTS:** *Better to think briefly about a single verse, than to skim through pages without absorbing anything.*
- **FALLING BEHIND:** *It's inevitable that you will occasionally miss a day. Don't be paralysed by guilt. Just start again.*
- **IT'S ABOUT DEVELOPING A LOVE RELATIONSHIP, NOT A LAW RELATIONSHIP** *Don't think that 'doing your quiet time' is an end in itself. The sign that your daily time with God is real is when you start to love Him more and serve Him more wholeheartedly.*

Tim Thornborough, *Explore Editor*

A goal for the year ahead

Reading: Proverbs 1 v 1-7 **Saturday** 1 January

Another new year slides in. You may be greeting it with fear ("I don't know how I'm going to get through"); boredom ("The same old routine starts all over again"); or excitement ("So many things to do and try").

What we feel often depends on our temperament, our circumstances and our stage in life.

Talk to the Lord about what your new year holds, and ask Him for the strength, wisdom and humility to serve Him in 2011.

What we all need

Read v 1-7

There may be many things that we need, but the Book of Proverbs is designed to help us grow in wisdom and understanding.

Which types of people does Solomon say need this book (v 4-5)?

What is his assessment of those who say they don't need it (v 7b)?

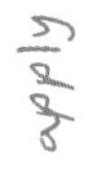

We can't say: "I just have a simple faith—this is far too complicated for me." Nor can we say we have "made it" as far as wisdom is concerned. Wrestling to understand the ways of the world with the mind of God is compulsory for all types of Christians. And those who reject this attitude risk being called "Fool" by God.

What wisdom really is

Read v 7

People of all cultures and times have tried to distil their observations on life into pithy, memorable sayings, in order to pass on an understanding of the world to others. Much of it is worthy, but the point that verse 7 makes is that, without God at its centre, human wisdom is never truly wise—just highly-educated foolishness.

The Lord God is the centre of all reality. Any system, or saying, that does not place Him at the centre is simply doing the bidding of the serpent, and will ultimately lead to false conclusions. Being in right relationship with God is the beginning of truly wise living.

What does it mean to "fear the Lord"?

What does it not mean?

If wisdom and understanding is for all, then above all in 2011, you must be committed to growth. There is no status quo in the kingdom of God. Rather like riding a bicycle—once we stop, we fall off!

Commit your year to the Lord, asking that you would humbly fear Him, and that you would grow in your understanding.

Keep going

Reading: Proverbs 1 v 7

Sunday 2 January

Think again about the poignant "theme verse" from the Book of Proverbs.

Read 1 v 7

The fear…

I remember talking with some shocked non-Christians after a dedication service, where the parents were made to promise that they would "bring up this child in the fear and knowledge of the Lord". They were livid, because it conjured up for them the image of the worst kind of religion: children being terrified of an angry God.

But that is not what is meant here. This kind of fear is healthy respect, not terror: just as one fears a flame, or a wild animal, so we know that God is to be treated with due reverence. As they say in Narnia: "Aslan is not a tame lion!"

…of the LORD…

And this is the key. True wisdom is not about some vague notion of "a God who is out there somewhere". No, this verse uses the covenant name of God (written in most Bibles in small capitals: LORD). He is the God who has revealed Himself through His dealings with His people. He is the God of Abraham, Isaac and Jacob. And He is the God who would ultimately reveal Himself in Jesus Christ.

And this God is not only a blazing fire, but is also filled with a burning love for His people, and a commitment not to judge, but to redeem them.

time out

Solomon was known for his wisdom, but who was the author of Proverbs unwittingly pointing towards?

Read Isaiah 11 v 2-3 and Luke 11 v 29-32.

…is the beginning of wisdom

"The beginning" can mean both the starting point and the chief goal or principle. What God reveals in His word about Himself, and about the meaning of fallen human behaviour, is the only sure guide to true understanding. That is why to reject it is to be content with darkness and not light. And what greater fool is there than the one who sits in the dark, when it is light outside, and convinces himself that he sees?

pray thru'

So, to be a grower in wisdom, rather than a sticker in foolishness, you need to be committed to humbly sitting under God's word day by day.

Ask the Lord, who is the source, focus and goal of all wisdom, to help you keep to your Bible reading this year; and that you will grow in understanding as a result.

GENESIS: No ordinary Joe

Reading: Genesis 37 v 1-11 **Monday** 3 January

Genesis 36 drew the curtain on Esau and his family. Attention now turns to Jacob's family, the line to whom God's covenant belongs, finally settled in the land of promise.

Read Genesis 37 v 1-11

Happy families?

How happy do you think Jacob's family was? What's the evidence of…

- *the description in v 2?*
- *Joseph's behaviour?*
- *Israel's (Jacob's) attitude (v 3)?*
- *the reaction of Joseph's brothers (v 4)?*

What has Jacob learned from his own family history (compare 25 v 28)?

The problem of favouritism in a family can be very acute, especially when inheritance is involved. Half-siblings and step-siblings in particular can feel left out. So it is with Joseph's brothers, especially those born to Bilhah and Zilpah, the servants of Rachel and Leah (v 2).

Joseph fuels the fire with his bad report of them—well received by Jacob, who loved Joseph (first son of his beloved wife Rachel) more than his brothers (v 3)! Worse, Jacob shows his favouritism by giving Joseph an immensely valuable robe. The brothers' hatred for Joseph, "daddy's boy" and snitch, is understandable—though not commendable.

time out

Jacob, of all people, should have known the catastrophic damage that favouritism can cause.

Read Romans 2 v 11 and James 2 v 1 and 9.

In what areas do you need to imitate your heavenly Father?

Arrogant

Joseph is also arrogant and almost wilfully stupid, telling his brothers not just one but two dreams about his own greatness (v 5-9). Even Jacob finds the second dream too much (v 10)— the idea of parents bowing down to their son was completely unthinkable. But Jacob knew that dreams can be true (**see Genesis 28 v 10-17**). Despite his annoyance, Jacob reflects on it all (v 11)—rightly, since the plans of God hinge around Joseph.

How would you have advised Joseph to behave? How could he keep godly without being a total pain to his ungodly brothers?

Moral uprightness needn't make us into prudes. Sometimes we need to be patient with people's moral failings.

The brothers' revenge

Reading: Genesis 37 v 12-36 **Tuesday** 4 January

Read Genesis 37 v 12-24

Nightmare for Joseph

How aware are Jacob and Joseph of Joseph's unpopularity?

What drives the brothers to contemplate murder (end of v 20)?

What might be behind Reuben's plan (see 35 v 22)?

Joseph's worst nightmare begins in a matter-of-fact way, when his unsuspecting father sends him out alone to his brothers, an errand that he willingly accepts (v 13-14). By now their hatred has become truly murderous (v 18). Joseph is nicknamed the "dreamer" (v 19), but his brothers intend to show that his dreams are empty (v 20).

Reuben, already in disgrace (35 v 22), might see an opportunity to redeem himself by rescuing his father's favourite (37 v 22b); or perhaps, as the eldest, he knows he will be held responsible by his father. He persuades the brothers only to throw Joseph into an empty cistern, from which Reuben hopes later to rescue him. But this leaves for the others the problem of what to do with him, since he can hardly be allowed to go home and tell his father about the outrage.

Read v 25-36

Solution for the brothers

What two things do the brothers gain from selling Joseph?

There's no material gain in killing Joseph, and there would be real problems with hiding the body (v 26). But selling him provides a both a profitable and a "moral" solution. Hands and consciences can both be clean (v 27), and pockets lined at the same time (v 28).

Reuben returns too late—despite his grief, he's now implicated and must go along with events (v 29-32). The brothers allow Jacob himself to invent the cover story—the sons merely have to agree with Jacob's conclusion that Joseph has been killed and eaten (v 33).

This story, like our lives, is full of "what ifs?". So many people could have behaved better. Yet be encouraged that God's plan is unstoppable. He uses Joseph's arrogance, his brothers' hatred and Jacob's favouritism, but also allows His people to go through intense personal suffering.

What should we learn from this?

A tale of two brothers

Reading: Genesis 38 — **Wednesday** 5 January

Proverbs 1 v 10-16 would have made good bedtime reading for Joseph's brothers generally, while **Proverbs 6 v 20-26** would have been especially helpful to Judah...

Read Genesis 38

Wilful neglect

- *What can we conclude about Judah in view of his marriage (v 2)?* ***Compare Genesis 24 v 3****.*
- *What's the reason for the deaths of Judah's two eldest sons (v 7, 10)?*
- *What does Judah appear to think the reason is (v 11)?*

By marrying a Canaanite Judah ignores his heritage, but God does not ignore his family. Judah's eldest son, Er, dies because of his wickedness (v 7). Then the second son, by seeking to deprive his widowed sister-in-law of heirs, also comes under judgment and dies (v 8-10). (God's command, implicit here, is later made explicit—**see Deuteronomy 25 v 5-6**.) Oblivious to the spiritual reasons for the death of his sons, Judah prefers to believe that his daughter-in-law is somehow "cursed".

Double standards

- *What is legitimate about the reason behind Tamar's dodgy plan?*
- *In what ways is Judah culpable?*

Judah himself provides an unwitting solution to his dilemma via Tamar's ingenuity. Knowing that Judah is holding out on her with regard to Shelah (v 14b), Tamar deliberately entices Judah into thinking she is a prostitute (v 15-16a). The morality is dubious—even though her claim to progeny in Judah's line is legitimate. When her pregnancy becomes obvious (v 24), she saves her life by exposing Judah's shameless double standards. Judah is forced to acknowledge her (comparative) righteousness (v 26).

! Pray to be delivered from your own double standards.

time out

The younger of Tamar's twins will be the ancestor of David (**see Ruth 4 v 18-22**). In Matthew's genealogy of Jesus (**Matthew 1**) five women are mentioned—two prostitutes (including Tamar), a foreigner, an adulteress and a single mum. It's hardly the sort of pedigree that most people would want to publicise! Is this a slur on these women or, given that the single mum is Mary, might there be another lesson?

Meanwhile, back in Egypt...

Reading: Genesis 39 **Thursday** 6 January

6

Read 39 v 1-6

Meteoric rise

As He didn't ignore Judah's family, so God doesn't ignore Joseph either. What's the outcome for Joseph?

How is God's promise to Abraham of blessing to the world being fulfilled here (v 5-6)?

In the years when Judah is experiencing his family problems, Joseph's fortunes almost irresistibly rise, not least because he acts with the kind of wisdom and integrity that Proverbs commends. God is with Joseph to bless him (v 2), just as He was with Judah to bring curses on his wicked family (38 v 7, 10). Moreover, through Joseph, Potiphar experiences a taste of the "world blessing" promised through Abraham (**compare v 5-6a with 12 v 3**).

Read v 7-23

Sudden downfall

How does Joseph's behaviour here compare with Judah's?

As Joseph continues to act with honour and integrity, what's the outcome for him now?

In his response to the attentions of Potiphar's wife, Joseph is exactly like the wise young man of **Proverbs 5 v 1-14**. To give in to the advances of Potiphar's wife would, in his view, be a sin against both God and Potiphar himself, who has trusted him with so much.

It is sometimes suggested that Joseph was unwise to enter the house when Potiphar's wife was there (v 11).

Does the text suggest Joseph was to blame (eg. v 10)?

What were Joseph's tactics when faced with repeated temptation?

Pray for the same practical wisdom when you are faced with temptation.

Although Joseph's behaviour continues to be exemplary, this time the outcome is an accusation of attempted rape (v 11-18) and unjust imprisonment by the outraged master he had tried to honour (v 20a)—provoking the question: *is God still with Joseph?*

What's the answer (v 21, 23)?

time out

We cannot assume that uprightness always results in good fortune, but we can be certain that the Lord is always "with" His people, and so it is always worth imitating Joseph, whatever the outcome may be.

More dreams

Reading: Genesis 40 **Friday** 7 January

7

Read the verses

Servant

What's the status of the two new prisoners?

*What extra responsibility is Joseph given (v 4, **compare 39 v 22-23**)?*

How does Joseph carry out his new responsibilities (v 6-7)?

Joseph must have suffered from stress, anxiety and boredom in prison. Then, when two new "guests" arrive—not menial servants, but honoured members of the court (**compare Nehemiah 2 v 1-9**)— Joseph has to serve them as well as run the prison (v 4a)! But an unexpected opportunity arises.

As in most cultures, the Egyptians recognised that dreams can be deeply significant, and so each official concludes that there must be a "message" involved in his vivid dream. But not knowing what it is, they are dejected when Joseph sees them the next day. Joseph's qualities, however, include sensitivity and compassion for those he serves (v 6). And when his enquiry about their mood discovers its cause, he can provide the answer, for he has had meaningful dreams of his own (**see 37 v 5-11**)!

Prophet

Who is it that will interpret these dreams (v 8)?

Joseph refuses the opportunity for self-promotion, but what opportunity does he seize at this point?

How does his godliness appear to be rewarded?

From the outset Joseph is at pains to point out that it is God, and not an interpreter, who really knows the meaning of dreams (v 8b, **see also 41 v 16**). And so what follows is not an example of divination or psychology, but prophecy.

In the deliverance of the cupbearer, however, Joseph sees an opportunity for his own deliverance from unjust imprisonment (v 14-15). In the event, the cupbearer forgets about Joseph—the man who served him in prison—as soon as he is restored to his high post (v 23). But if Joseph had promoted himself as the interpreter of dreams—who knows?—he may have made a greater impression on the cupbearer and got out of jail earlier.

time out

It can always be argued that ungodly behaviour pays greater dividends. That's what makes it so appealing?

How would you argue against that?

From prison to palace

Reading: Genesis 41 v 1-40

Saturday 8 January

Read the passage

A long wait

What does verse 1 reveal about what Joseph had to endure?

What would you be thinking in his shoes?

time out

Joseph presumably believed God had a plan for his life, as should we. But what was he to do when for two years he couldn't discern the plan?

What does this true story reveal about…

- *the world's most powerful man (v 8a)?*
- *the finest minds of the day (v 8b)?*
- *God's providential planning to get Joseph precisely where He wanted him to be (v 9-13)?*

Pharaoh is a man with extensive and absolute power but also a troubled mind. Once again the answer to the mystery lies not in the diviners (v 8), but with the Divinity (v 16). The prison incident—now a distant memory for Joseph and initially not even that for the cupbearer— proves to have been an essential part of God's plan, giving Joseph a spokesman in Pharaoh's court. The cupbearer's testimony quickly establishes Joseph's credentials (v 10-13) and he is duly sent for (v 14).

A rapid elevation

What is Pharaoh's verdict on Joseph (v 38-39)?

The "discerning and wise man" (v 33) needed to implement Joseph's suggested 14-year national strategy is not hard to find, since even Pharaoh can see that the Spirit of God is in the man who stands in front of him (v 38-39). So Joseph is elevated from prison to a position second only to Pharaoh himself (v 40).

God used one man, filled with His wisdom, as the instrument of a great deliverance. Yet His plan was to save not just Egypt, Joseph, or even Joseph's family, but the world—when He would again use one man filled with His wisdom (**see Matthew 12 v 42; 1 Corinthians 1 v 30**).

When life seems to be going nowhere, despite our desire to do things for God, we needn't fret about being sidelined. Pray for patience in situations where nothing seems to be happening, and wisdom to seize the opportunity to serve God when it comes.

Sound advice from Dad

Reading: Proverbs 1 v 8-19 **Sunday** 9 January

Proverbs often adopts a "voice". Here it is the voice of parents instructing their children in the way of godliness.

Read v 8-19

Armed robbery—avoid it!

Read v 11-15

Not many *Explore* readers will face this particular temptation, but the word of God is for all people at all time. There are many decent parents who have watched with tears in their eyes as their children have taken up lives of crime and violence. And this applies not just to street violence and mugging—there are plenty of bloodthirsty robbers in "polite society" as well.

What is the attraction of this kind of life to a young person (v 13-14)?

pray thru'

Pray for Christian parents as they try to instill godly wisdom in their children. It is especially hard for single parents living in tough neighbourhoods.

Is there any help you can offer to a parent with a child or teenager who is in danger of falling into this kind of world?

The pull of the crowd

Read v 10

We neglect the power of the crowd to influence us at our peril. It is so much easier to "go with the flow" and ignore the evil implications of what we do *en masse*. There is friendship and good company, even among the wicked—sometimes even altruism ("let us share one purse", v 14).

Think about when you are most vulnerable to being influenced by the crowd: is it at work, among friends, or even at church!?

The end of all wickedness

Read v 18-19

What argument is used to turn these children away from evil (v 18-19)?

Running right through Proverbs is this one assumption: **those who sin will pay a price**. So those who give themselves over to a life of wickedness are working towards their own self destruction. This is wisdom informed by the fear of the LORD, who is the Judge of all men. Human wisdom will say: "Don't get caught". Godly wisdom says: "You will always be caught, because God our Judge sees everything."

Sin always pays a wage (**see Romans 6 v 23**). Worldly wisdom offers immediate gratification, with no thought to the future. Godly wisdom knows that we have a whole life to live, and after that to face judgment.

Are you guilty of "short-termism" in your behaviour? You will reap the consequences—in this life and the next.

BIBLE IN A YEAR: **GENESIS 23-24 • ROMANS 8 v 22-39**

God's man in charge

Reading: Genesis 41 v 41-57 **Monday** 10 January

Joseph's fortunes have changed dramatically...

Read verses 41-57

Fruitfulness

- *What do you think is the reason for Joseph's new name and wife?*
- *How long has it taken Joseph to travel from slave to Pharaoh's second-in-command? (**See verse 46; compare 37 v 2.**)*
- *Look at the Hebrew names Joseph gives to his sons (v 51-52). What does he forget and what does he remember?*

If Joseph is to be co-ruler over Egypt (v 44), he must become culturally Egyptian, hence the new name and Egyptian wife (v 45a). Only then can he begin his duties (v 45b).

time out

Joseph's elevation from prison was no time to be picky. His change of name had to be accepted with good grace, although the gift of a pagan wife might have presented him with more difficulties!

- *Are there times when we should similarly swallow some of our principles? Is it always right to stick by them? When should we be flexible and when should we stand firm?*

Read 1 Corinthians 9 v 19-23.

Joseph has used well the 13 years from his enslavement to this "moment of destiny" (**compare Judah, ch. 38**). The prophetic dream of seven abundant years has come true, enabling Joseph to gather "grain mountains" so huge it isn't even worth keeping a tally of them (v 47-49).

Joseph is personally fruitful as well, gaining two sons (v 50). They are given Hebrew names: "Forget"—perhaps in the sense of forgetting the past—and "Fruitful", reflecting the blessing Joseph has so remarkably received from God (v 52).

- *What do you need to forget (and forgive) today?*
- *What goodness from God do you need to remember (and thank Him for)?*

Famine

Then the years of famine arrive "just as Joseph had said" (v 54, compare v 30-32)—these words reminding us again that, despite the widespread and desperate situation (v 57), God is firmly in charge.

Pray for confidence in God's sovereignty, both in your individual circumstances and when you look at the world scene.

"Near-miss" reunion

Reading: Genesis 42 **Tuesday** 11 January

Back in Canaan...

Read Genesis 42 v 1-20

Disaster looms

What's the evidence here that the journey to Egypt was an act of desperation?

The headstrong, wayward sons might have been good in a fight, but Jacob clearly feels that they are useless in a fix (v 1)! Although a trip to Egypt seems the obvious solution, the brothers are evidently reluctant to go, and Jacob, wary of further disaster, keeps back the remaining son of his beloved Rachel.

Why the pretence and harsh words from Joseph, do you think?

Joseph's harsh words may result more from his own confusion than a desire to humiliate his brothers. Indeed, it's only when Joseph sees them bowing down before him that he remembers the dreams that caused his original problems (v 9a, **compare 37 v 10**).

But having started the masquerade, Joseph must keep it up. Thus the brothers are accused of spying (v 9b-12). When Joseph hears about Benjamin (v 13), he sets about "persuading" his brothers (v 14-17) to bring Jacob's youngest son—his own closest sibling—before this "God-fearing" Egyptian (v 18-20).

Read verses 21-38

Disaster strikes

What does the brothers' conversation show (v 21-23)?

What reveals Joseph's good intentions?

Joseph's tears reveal his true feelings towards his brothers. He seems genuinely moved by the signs of their slowly awakening consciences. Now he plans to test his brothers further. By returning their silver with the grain, he turns their fear into despondency and guilt (v 28) and then, ultimately, into panic (v 35)—will they keep the money and once again lie to their father?

They do neither, but when they arrive home, Jacob refuses to allow the deal to go through, even when Reuben offers two of his own sons as hostage for Benjamin (v 36-38). And so Joseph's longed-for reunion is postponed indefinitely.

time out

Praise God for the gift of conscience. Though the pangs of a guilty conscience can cause us great suffering, the purpose of this gift is to bring us to God for confession, repentance, forgiveness and reconciliation. **Read Psalm 32.**

The return

Reading: Genesis 43 **Wednesday** 12 January

Read Genesis 43 v 1-15

Hesitation and delay

Jacob is torn between wanting to protect Benjamin by keeping him at home and the urgent need to get more food from Egypt, which means sending Benjamin there to fulfil Joseph's demand (v 5).

- *How does Jacob's anxiety show itself (v 6)?*
- *What's his main strategy for ensuring Benjamin's safe return (v 11-12)?*
- *Look at Jacob's opening words in v 11 and his closing words in v 14. What's his state of mind?*
- *How much faith in God's sovereignty does he truly have, do you think (v 14)?*

Jacob is facing his worst nightmare—the loss of the only surviving son (as he sees it) of his beloved wife Rachel. He responds to the stress by lashing out petulantly and unjustifiably at his other sons (v 6), by setting things up as favourably as possible for the family delegation in Egypt, and finally, by descending into fatalism—"If I am bereaved, I am bereaved". In the midst of all this, his words about God in verse 14 sound more like a desperate last resort than a confident assurance of God's sovereignty.

apply

- *Do Jacob's reactions to his stressful situation sound familiar?*
- *How do other parts of Scripture show a better way to respond? Read* ***Philippians 4 v 4-7****, for instance.*

Read Genesis 43 v 16-34

Welcome and feasting

Ironically, Jacob's sons now fear the very thing they inflicted on Joseph—enslavement (v 18). Their story about the silver is not completely truthful but Genesis faithfully records it, "warts and all". The steward is "in", not only on the truth, but on the underlying spiritual realities. "Your God," he assures them, has been at work (v 23a). And Joseph is both deeply moved at this reunion (v 30) and clearly enjoying himself (v 33-34).

time out

There are so many "what ifs" with this story. What if Joseph hadn't been so prude-ish, his father so divisive, his brothers so jealous? Certainly, many complications would have been avoided had everyone done what was right. Yet God's sovereignty overrules entirely!

- Praise God—this is true for you as well!

Insight

Reading: Genesis 44

Thursday 13 January

Read the passage

Character test

Why do you think Joseph doesn't reveal himself to his brothers during the feast?

What is he hoping to reveal by insisting that Benjamin stays in Egypt as his slave (v 17)?

Joseph wisely realises that his brothers *have not yet been revealed to themselves* (**compare 42 v 21-24a**). So he sets them a true test of character—will they sacrifice another brother to save themselves? Joseph's special cup is hidden in Benjamin's sack and, shortly after they leave, the steward is sent in pursuit. The words given to the steward (v 5) heighten the sense of divine retribution and also continue to mask Joseph's Hebrew identity (compare v 15).

Guilt revelation

Although the brothers are absolutely sure of their innocence (v 7-9), the discovery of the cup uncovers a deeper issue—they know they are guilty of a much greater crime (v 16) and so they admit they collectively deserve punishment.

*What is significant about Judah's leadership here? (**Compare 37 v 26-27.**)*

Judah again rises to the occasion (**see also 43 v 8-10**). He points out the devastating impact on Jacob if Benjamin fails to come home (v 27-31) and offers himself as a substitute to spare his father's misery (v 34). It was Judah of course who came up with the plot to sell Joseph into slavery (37 v 26-27) and caused his father's misery over the first loss of a son. The subsequent guilt might also explain why Judah left home for a prolonged period (chapter 38). But now he is determined to spare his father any more misery, even at the cost of his own future (v 33). And thus the full impact of the last 20 or more years is revealed.

Guilt corrodes our lives and relationships. A frank confession is what's needed. Think carefully before you speak to someone because sometimes confession can simply open old wounds, not heal them! But you must certainly bring the matter to the Lord.

Talk to God now about those things which still make you feel guilty. **Read 1 John 1 v 7.**

Happy ending

Reading: Genesis 45 | **Friday** 14 January

14

Read the passage

Revelation

*Why does Joseph's composure fall apart at this point (v 1-2; **compare 44 v 33-34**)?*

How does Joseph reassure his terrified brothers that they will not be harmed?

How is Joseph's understanding of all that has happened to him linked to the promises God made to Abraham (v 7)?

Joseph can no longer hide his feelings or his true identity, most likely because of the poignant reminder of his father's grief, or perhaps the remarkable sight of Judah's transformation from the jealous, vengeful schemer who enslaved his brother into the responsible and courageous protector of his family.

The brothers' emotions are very different since the young man they sold as a slave now has the power to destroy them all. But Joseph reassures them that there's no need for distress or self-recrimination (v 5a). Since all this time God has been at work to save the lives of this family to whom so much has been promised (v 5b-8), why would Joseph now set about destroying them?

"In all things God works for the good of those who love him" (Romans 8 v 28). Easy to say, but often hard to see, except on rare occasions like this.

Pray for patience when you cannot see how things could possibly work out "for the good".

Reunion

How does God continue to open up the way for Joseph's family to be rescued from famine (v 16-20)?

Joseph plans that Jacob and the entire family will live in Egypt—in Goshen—not only to be near Joseph, but also to survive the famine, most of which is still to come (v 10-11). And Pharaoh not only permits this, but goes out of his way to welcome and provide abundantly for Joseph's family (v 16-23). Jacob's initial scepticism shows how demoralised he has become, but what he sees convinces him and his spirit revives (v 26-28).

If God's "amazing grace" has brought you safe this far, trust that His grace will bring you "home".

Jacob's move

Reading: Genesis 46 v 1-30

Saturday 15 January

So far "the account of Jacob" (37 v 2) seems to have been about Joseph, his son. But now the focus shifts firmly back to Jacob (or Israel) himself.

Reassurance

Read Genesis 46 v 1-7

Why does God need to tell Jacob not to be afraid to go to Egypt (v 2-3)? ***Compare Genesis 15 v 12-16.***

Jacob is leaving the land promised to Abraham. Since God's words in Genesis 15 v 13 must have been known to Jacob, he would also have known that this move would bring oppression to his descendants. Doubtless this is why God reassures him in a vision (v 2-4)—one day the land will be re-entered, even though Jacob himself will be long-since dead.

time out

The more Jacob understands of God's big plan for His people and how things will ultimately turn out, the more he can trust God, as Joseph did, through dark times. Perhaps we find it hard to trust God when things get difficult because we understand poorly or we don't remind ourselves of God's big plan for His people. **Read Ephesians 3 v 7-13.**

Read Genesis 46 v 8-30

Roll call

Why do you think the direct descendants of Jacob are listed like this at the point when the family is moving to Egypt? What's the connection with God's promises to Abraham?

The "thirty-three" offspring of Jacob (v 15) seem in fact to be only thirty-two (Er and Onan being dead, v 12), but probably include Jacob himself (see bracketed note, v 8). However, the important point is that in the fourth generation from Abraham, God's chosen family are finally becoming numerous. God's promise of innumerable descendants of Abraham (**Genesis 15 v 4-5**)—as well as His prediction about relocation to Egypt (15 v 13-16)—is being fulfilled.

Salvation has come to Abraham's family but in time this salvation will become a prison from which they need saving again.

Read **1 Thessalonians 4 v 13-18** and praise God for our *eternal* salvation through Jesus Christ.

Who is this man?

Reading: Psalm 110 **Sunday** 16 January

On first reading this is a somewhat strange psalm. It falls into two parts (v 1-3 and 4-7), and each part starts with a statement from God to someone else. But who is it? The answer to that question means that this is one of the most quoted parts of the Old Testament in the New!

Conquering King

Read v 1-3

David is the author: so who is God talking to?

- *What is his current privilege? (v 1)*
- *What has he got to look forward to? (v 2)*
- *What picture does v 3 bring to mind?*

Of course, the psalm is talking about Jesus—David's "Lord" whom the LORD will make both conqueror and King. It is talking about His return to God's presence after being raised from the dead, and His being seated at God's right hand. The "sitting" signifies that His work is finished!

- *What was the work that Jesus has now finished?*
- *Where is Jesus now; and what is He waiting for?*

time out

We live in a time of waiting: the work of Christ is finished, but He is yet to be revealed as Lord of all—we must trust that He "rules in the midst of his enemies" (v 2b).

- *Do you find that difficult? How would you answer someone who says: "There is no God: the world is full of injustice, hatred and evil."*

Priest and Judge

Read v 4-7

- *What has God promised to Jesus (v 4)? What does that mean?*

Melchizedek was a king and priest of Salem (later to become Jerusalem), who gave a blessing to Abraham (**see Genesis 14 v 18-20**). But the bestowal of priesthood on Jesus shows us what He came to do: to rule the world, and to open a way back into the presence of God for us.

- *But what will Jesus do then (v 5-6)? And when?*
- *How is His humanity shown (v 7)?*

time out

A day is coming when all wrongs will be put right: permanently.

- *Are you ready for that day yet? Have your friends, neighbours, workmates, family been warned of its coming?*

Check out some or all of the New Testament references to this psalm: **Matthew 22 v 41-46; Acts 2 v 34-35; 1 Corinthians 15 v 25; Hebrews 1 v 13; 5 v 6; 6 v 17-20; ch. 7; 10 v 12-13.**

Settling down

Reading: Genesis 46 v 31 – 47 v 12

Read 46 v 31 – 47 v 6

Separation

- *Why does Joseph insist on an occupation for his family that the Egyptians find detestable (46 v 34)?*
- *How is Joseph's plan for his family in Egypt shaped by God's promise to Abraham (15 v 13-16).*

As one who knows Egyptian ways, Joseph naturally handles the negotiations with Pharaoh as to where his family will live. However, his purpose is not just to secure the best land for them (47 v 6), but also to keep his family separate from the Egyptians (46 v 34b), so that they will not be assimilated into Egyptian ways. Joseph is thinking ahead to the time when God will call his descendants to return to the land of Canaan. They will be reluctant to go if they have come to feel "at home" in Egypt.

Read Philippians 3 v 17-21.

Christians similarly look forward to a day when God will call us into His heavenly "promised land".

- *Does that prospect thrill you? Or do you feel too much "at home" in this world?*
- *Will you be distinctive as one of God's people, even if that makes you "detestable" to unbelievers?*

- *What action do you need to take to avoid being assimilated into this world?*

Read Genesis 47 v 7-12

Blessing

- *What's remarkable about this scene?*
- *Why does Pharaoh show Jacob such respect?*
- *How is God's promise about a blessing to all nations yet again being fulfilled?*

Here before the absolute ruler of a great world power stands Jacob—malnourished, unshaven, strangely dressed. Yet Jacob's age and experience are clearly striking (v 8) and give him the right to reverse the normal protocols (**compare Hebrews 7 v 7**).

Long life hasn't brought great happiness for Jacob. Yet as the inheritor of God's promise of world blessing—together with Abraham and Isaac—it's Jacob who blesses Pharaoh.

Don't expect an easy ride, just because you serve the Almighty God.

Pray that your own difficulties may build up your faith so that you too may "bless" others.

Prosperity and posterity

Reading: Genesis 47 v 13-31 **Tuesday** 18 January

Read Genesis 47 v 13-27

Prosperity

What does Joseph take from the Egyptians in return for the gift of life?

v 14:

v 16

v 20-21:

Do you think Joseph was unduly harsh in his treatment of the Egyptians?

In God's providence, Joseph's handling of the famine brings Pharaoh unimagined prosperity. He takes the Egyptians' money (v 14-15), livestock (v 16-17) and finally their land and liberty (v 18-21)! Only the priesthood escapes with their land because Pharaoh already supplies them with food (v 22). The social structures of Egypt are permanently changed (v 26). Joseph also introduces a 20% tax on produce. It seems a very raw deal, but as the people themselves recognise, Joseph has saved their lives.

The others who prosper are the family of Israel (v 27). Unlike the Egyptians, they actually acquire property in this period—doubtless due to Joseph's protection.

time out

The Bible has a clear message for the superpower nations of this world. Read the words of God to another, later ruler of a world superpower in **Isaiah 45 v 1-7, 16-17, 22-25.**

time out

What do we learn about…

- *God's power over superpowers (v 1-3)?*
- *God's purposes in raising them up (v 4, v 5-7)?*
- *God's attitude towards them (v 16 and 24)?*
- *God's attitude to His people (v 17 and 25)?*
- *God's desire for the nations (v 22)?*

Read Isaiah 60 v 1-12.

What will the nations do for God's people?

What will God's people do for the nations (v 2-3)?

In Joseph's day, these truths were already being worked out in the relationship between Egypt and the family of Israel.

What lessons are there for us?

Read verses 28-31

Posterity

What must Joseph do to show his father "kindness and faithfulness"?

Despite his prosperity in Egypt, Jacob knows that the future lies in the land of the promise, hence his urgent wish to be buried there.

What dominates your thinking? Immediate prosperity or future blessing? Read **1 Peter 1 v 3-5**: repent if needed and give thanks.

BIBLE IN A YEAR: **GENESIS 43-45 • ROMANS 15 v 1-13**

Right reversal

Reading: Genesis 48

Wednesday 19 January

Read the passage

New generation

- *What status does Jacob confer on Joseph's two eldest sons (v 5)?*
- *Why, do you think? (See v 11 and v 7.)*
- *What family pattern is repeated here (v 12-19)? (**Compare 25 v 23 and 17 v 18-21.**)*

Joseph knows Jacob's end is near (v 1), and also that there is unfinished business. Manasseh and Ephraim have a special place in Jacob's affections (v 11), and they will have a special place in God's plans, so Joseph brings them with him. After reminding Joseph of the covenant promise (v 3-4), Jacob declares that these two particular grandsons are to be treated as his own sons (v 5-6). Verse 7 suggests he also sees them as children of Rachel, who died prematurely in childbirth.

Joseph arranges the boys so that his father's right hand will naturally find the older (v 13), but, to his annoyance (v 17), his father crosses his arms to bless them (v 14), thus reversing the privilege of the firstborn. But though this might seem to be the result of failing eyesight or the confusion of old age, it is actually deliberate (v 19). Remembering Jacob's own background (25 v 23), however, this shouldn't surprise us.

time out

Read 1 Chronicles 5 v 1-2.

Jacob's blessing reverses the rights of the firstborn twice. Joseph is given this status over Reuben, and Ephraim over Manasseh.

- *Why does God keep reversing the right of the firstborn?*

See Romans 9 v 10-16.

Same promises

The phrase "he blessed Joseph" (v 15) encompasses Joseph's two sons as well (**see 1 Chronicles 5 v 1-2**). They are blessed as themselves sons of Abraham, Isaac and Jacob (v 16b), and inheritors of the blessing of fruitfulness (v 16c). As for Joseph, God will be with him (v 21; **compare 26 v 3**), and will take him and his people ("you" and "your" are plural here) back to the land of promise (**compare 15 v 16**).

pray thru'

Praise God that His mercy and compassion do not depend on man's desire or effort.

The verdict: part 1

Reading: Genesis 49 v 1-15 **Thursday** 20 January

20

Jacob's sons assemble to listen to their father's final words...

Read Genesis 49 v 1-15

- *How appropriate is it to describe Jacob's words to his sons as "blessings"? What is really going on here (see v 28)?*
- *Which blessing stands out? Why?*

Reuben (v 3-4):

- *How had Reuben at first excelled (v 3)?*
- *Why would Reuben "no longer excel" (v 4; **compare 35 v 22**)?*

As firstborn, the rights of seniority and leadership were his. But Reuben's character and morals failed him utterly. So he would "no longer excel" as the firstborn should.

Simeon and Levi (v 5-7):

- *What was their failing? (**See 34 v 25-29.**)*
- *In what ways did Jacob's "blessing" fit their crime (v 6a, 7b)?*

Simeon and Levi's massacre in revenge for Dinah's rape was a disproportionate act of violent rage, not justice. So the inseparable avengers were to be ostracised (v 6a) and separated from each other (v 7b).

Judah (v 8-12):

- *How has Judah shown leadership among his brothers? (**See 43 v 8-10; 44 v 18-34.**)*
- *How does Jacob's blessing for Judah change in verse 10?*

Judah's blessing (v 8-9) is initially addressed to him personally. Judah *(sounds like "praise")* will be praised by his brothers as the conqueror of the family's enemies. But there is much more to this blessing than the others: a coming Ruler to whom the nations truly belong (v 10b) will bring an appropriate climax to Judah's rule (**compare Ezekiel 21 v 25-27**).

Zebulun and Issachar (v 13-15):

Even the quiet, unremarkable one and the tough but lazy one get a mention.

These strangely named "blessings" are, in fact, verdicts "appropriate" (v 28) to each son.

pray thru'

This "mixed bunch" were the foundational members of God's people (**see Revelation 21 v 12**). God's family now is also made up of gifted yet flawed people, whom He nonetheless uses for His own purposes and glory.

- Praise God that He can use you through, and in spite of, your flaws and failings.

The verdict: part 2

Reading: Genesis 49 v 16-28 **Friday** 21 January

21

The verdict of Jacob on his sons continues:

Read the passage

Which of these verdicts stands out, and why?

Dan (v 16-17):

What was good and what was bad about Dan?

The vindicator of Rachel (30 v 6), Dan had the potential to be his people's judge (v 16), but was also capable of causing unexpected disaster (v 17; **compare Judges 18**). No wonder Jacob slips in a prayer for "salvation" (v 18—"deliverance" in NIV: the word that gives us the name Joshua/Jesus!).

Gad (v 19):

As a border tribe, Gad would often be raided but not easily overcome.

Asher (v 20):

The "fat cat" of the family, Asher would not only provide luxuries for Israel but enjoy them. But this life of luxury would sap the will to fight (**see Judges 5 v 17**).

Naphtali (v 21):

Destined to be a tribe of beautiful character, Naphtali rose to the occasion under the leadership of Barak (**see Judges 4 v 6-10**).

Joseph (v 22-26):

What's the reason for Joseph's steadfastness of character in hostile circumstances?

Unsurprisingly, Joseph gets a big mention, but Jacob's words here focus just as much on "the Mighty One of Jacob" (v 24b), the one behind Joseph's character and good fortune—the "Shepherd" and "Rock" and God of his fathers, who had blessed him abundantly (v 25).

time out

How does Jacob's description of Joseph—"the prince among his brothers" (v 26)—anticipate Christ Himself?

Read Romans 8 v 29 and Hebrews 2 v 11-12, 14 – 3 v 1.

Benjamin (v 27):

Jacob's description of his youngest (possibly spoilt) son as "a ravenous wolf" was proved true by the events of **Judges 19 – 21**, though Moses would have a kinder verdict (**Deuteronomy 33 v 12**).

pray thru'

In a "report" on your life, what phrase might God use to best sum you up?

Too easily influenced by friends? Much unfulfilled potential? Too prone to fighting? Too interested in money? Lazy toad? Great worker? Other: __________

What will you do about it?

The death of Jacob

Reading: Genesis 49 v 29 – 50 v 14 **Saturday** 22 January

Inevitably, what first began with Adam back in Genesis 5 v 5, and has recurred in every generation since, is about to take place yet again…

Read Genesis 49 v 29-33

Death

What lies behind Jacob's final request (v 29-32)?

How is his death described (v 33)? What does this tell us?

As deaths go, this is a good one. Jacob is ready to depart this life. He knows where he wants his final resting place to be—in the cave purchased by Abraham from the Hittites (the only part of the land of promise that Abraham ever owned), where the other patriarchs and their wives are buried. This is not just the expression of an exile's longing for his fondly-remembered homeland, but the outworking of Jacob's continued faith in God's promises to his ancestors. Having thus given his final instructions, Jacob lies back and dies.

Jacob is "gathered to his people"—it's not just a euphemism for death, but also reflects the tremendous truth about death for God's people—**see Hebrews 11 v 8-10, 13-16**.

Read Genesis 50 v 1-14

Grief

What is Joseph's response, as a man of faith, to the death of his father?

Joseph is distraught (50 v 1). Death is still an "enemy" (**1 Corinthians 15 v 26**), and grief is appropriate (**see John 11 v 32-35**).

time out

Read 1 Thessalonians 4 v 13.

What's the right balance between grief and hope?

Pray for those who mourn, especially over the death of a parent.

Burial

What shows the high regard in which Jacob, as father of Joseph, was held?

v 3:

v 6:

v 7-9:

Jacob's burial with "full honours" includes embalming by Joseph's own physicians (v 2-3a), an official period of mourning equivalent to a state funeral (v 3b), Pharaoh's personal permission for Joseph to leave Egypt (v 4-6), a huge escort to Canaan (v 7-9) and a lavish funeral ceremony that makes a lasting impression on the locals (v 10-11).

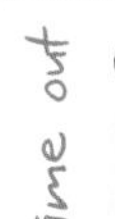

How might your funeral give glory to God and expression to the gospel?

And finally...

Reading: Genesis 50 v 15-26

Sunday 23 January

23

Read the passage

What thinking leads Joseph's brothers to send these (probably invented) instructions from their father?

What thinking leads Joseph to treat them with grace?

Guilt

Joseph's brothers remain in thrall to their guilt. With Jacob dead, the terrible thought occurs that Joseph might have waited for this moment to take his revenge (v 15). Perhaps this is how they would act in Joseph's shoes. Certainly, blood-letting among siblings after the death of their father is far from unknown. The fact is, Joseph's grace is incomprehensible to his brothers, because grace is incomprehensible to human nature generally.

Grace

So what makes Joseph so different? It's his unswerving trust in God's sovereignty (v 19-20). Joseph is free of vengeance because he leaves all matters of justice and punishment to the supreme Judge of all (v 19). Even if his own feelings were otherwise, how could he act as if he were God (v 19)? Joseph is also free of bitterness because he accepts that God allowed his suffering for a greater good—the saving of many lives (v 20).

pray thru'

Is your life still shaped by guilt, like the brothers? Or by grace through faith in God's sovereignty, like Joseph?

Take time to talk to God about these things.

time out

"You intended to harm me, but God intended it for good to accomplish what is now being done, the saving of many lives."

How does Joseph foreshadow Christ? ***See Acts 2 v 22-24, 36; 4 v 27-28.***

Faith

Characteristically, Joseph's last act is one of faith. Certain that God will one day bring His people out of Egypt to the land of the promise, Joseph makes his "brothers" (ie: relatives) promise that his bones will be taken with God's people on the great journey (**see Exodus 13 v 19; Hebrews 11 v 22**).

pray thru'

"This world is not my home," says an old American song, "I'm just a-passing through".

Looking at how you live, would people guess this to be true for you, by the way you spend your time, money and leisure?

Philippians: True fellowship

Reading: Philippians 1 v 1-5 **Monday** 24 January

If you had been unjustly imprisoned, what kind of letters would you be writing? If it were me, they would be filled with self-pity and rage. But Paul's letter is filled with joy and thanksgiving...

Read v 1-2

Slaves and saints

How do Paul and TImothy describe themselves and the Philippian Christians they write to?

"Grace and peace" was a standard greeting in the ancient world—how is it filled with so much more significance for Christians?

apply

Paul was an apostle and Timothy a leader, but they describe themselves as servants, or slaves. This is Jesus' call to anyone who wants to be great in the kingdom of God. **See Mark 10 v 43-44.**

Likewise, the word "saints" is not just reserved for extra-special believers, but describes all true Christians—dedicated to God's service, made pure and holy by the grace they have received from God through Jesus Christ.

So, is that how you see yourself? Made holy by Christ to be a slave to others, for His sake?

The fellowship of the King

Read v 3-5

Think of some of the things that separated Paul from the Philippians.

But what was it that held them together?

They were separated by **distance** (Paul was imprisoned, probably in Rome—**see 4 v 22**). By **race** (Paul was Jewish, most of them probably Greeks) Also by **time** (it was a number of years since he had been to Philippi). They were separated by **status**—Paul was a great apostle from a wealthy Pharisee family: they were "ordinary Christians", many of them from humble birth.

But the remarkable thing is that God had joined them together in a miraculous way through the gospel. They had true fellowship with one another that united them in a shared identity, and made them partners in a shared purpose.

What was that purpose (v 5)?

If our aim is to find true fellowship, it will always evade us—our differences will get in the way, and we will be disappointed with one another. But when our aim is to work together for the gospel—bringing the good news of Jesus Christ to others—then we will find a fellowship of sacrificial love that fills us with joy.

pray thru'

For many Christians, the happiest time of their lives has been when they have been working together on a mission or camp where they have laboured together for the gospel.

Pray that your own church, and others you know, would experience that same joy in united service.

True faith

Reading: Philippians 1 v 3-8 **Tuesday** 25 January

25

Some people are always starting things and then giving them up. The house is littered with half-done Do-it-Yourself projects, half-read books and the remnants of sudden enthusiasms that were dropped when the initial thrill subsided.

Read v 3-6

God's work

What is Paul confident about in v 6?

What gives him this confidence?

People are fickle, but God is not. Paul is bursting with confidence because he knows that the thriving of the Philippian Christians doesn't depend on their own determination, but on the grace of God working in them.

time out

You do understand this, don't you? If you are a Christian today, it is because God has done a work in your heart. And if He has started that work in you, you can be absolutely 100% sure that He will finish it. **Read John 10 v 27-29.**

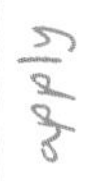

You may think that you are a pretty poor Christian. Your prayer life is weak. You feel that you disappoint Jesus often. Sometimes you even think you would like to give up! Remember that God will *never* give up on you. Remember that you are massively valuable to Him. Jesus paid the price of His blood for you, and will make you perfect when He returns.

Our work

Read v 5-8

What are the signs that God is truly at work in the lives of Paul's readers?

How does this make the apostle feel?

When God works in someone's heart through the gospel, you start to see outward changes. The bond of fellowship with other Christians is one sign. A desire to help tell others about Christ is another. The fact that you persevere through difficult times is a third. The Philippians showed all these marks of a genuine work of God in them. No wonder Paul is bubbling over with joy and love for them—even when he's in chains!

Note that the outward things are not what makes someone a real Christian. But they are the sign that God is at work in us. In other words, our work for God shows that God has worked in us.

So where does your Christian service spring from? Do you do it from a sense of duty or because God has filled your heart with gratitude for what He has done for you?

Talk to God about your answer…

True prayer

Reading: Philippians 1 v 9-11

Wednesday 26 January

26

We pray for David's auntie who is in hospital, and that Gemma would find a new job, and that Robbie would pass his school exams…

❓ *How similar is this to the kind of prayers that you offer to God on your own, or when you meet with others to pray?*

Read v 9-11

❓ *What kinds of things is Paul praying for? Does that surprise you?*

❓ *Can you spot four things (at least) that Paul wants to see develop in his readers?*

❓ *What is Paul praying will be the outcome of all this growth (v 11)?*

apply

It's natural to talk to the Lord about the specific problems we face. It's normal to pray for practical needs. It's just that our prayers so often stop there, and don't go on to the more important things that we should be concerned about. We would love David's aunt to get better, Gemma to get a new job and Robbie to get straight A's, but it is way more important that they grow in love, understanding, discernment and holiness.

True love

It's not that they were loveless before—they were filled with love for Paul, for each other and for others. But Paul prays that their love would grow in "knowledge and all discernment" (ESV).

❓ *Why does love need to be discerning? And what "knowledge" will make love better?*

Love, contrary to popular notions, is not just a gushy feeling towards someone. It is a desire to actively seek the best for others. So love for a believer is intimately bound up with the will of God and the gospel. We will only know how to do good to and for others if we understand what is *really* good for them. And only God knows that. Paul's prayer is that they would know God's mind, so that they would love more intelligently.

Discerning love is driven by our understanding of God and what He is doing in the world. It means that Christians will **give** differently—being concerned for spiritual hunger as well as physical hunger. Christians will **comfort** differently—not just tea and sympathy, but encouraging people to see the eternal perspective to their problems.

❓ *Can you think of another practical illustration of this principle?*

pray thru'

It's time to follow Paul's example. So pray Paul's prayer for your church, your friends and your family.

❗ And pray the same things for yourself.

❓ *How will your love grow more discerning this week?*

True sight

Reading: Philippians 1 v 12-18 **Thursday** 27 January

No one can accuse Paul of being a pessimist! He's sat shackled between two Roman soldiers awaiting trial, and he's writing a letter telling his friends how filled with joy he is...

Is this just bravado, incurable optimism or a failure to grasp the truth of the situation? Actually, it's none of the above...

Read v 12-18

Seeing clearly

- *What is Paul thrilled about?*
- *In addition to his imprisonment, what other things might have made Paul upset?*
- *What is the most important thing that Paul is focused on?*

No doubt some people would think him insane—but actually Paul sees the bigger issues more clearly. He loves others with discernment (v 10), and knows that the most important thing in the world is that people hear about Jesus Christ, and the gospel message about Him. His circumstances and personal comfort are irrelevant in the light of this truth. And amazingly, God has used the "disaster" of Paul's imprisonment to bring more and more people to hear about Christ.

He spoke about Christ to the soldiers who were guarding him—and the other Christians were made bold and courageous by Paul's example.

apply

We should not be surprised by this! Our God is an expert at working out His plans for good, even when evil men are doing their worst. **Read Genesis 50 v 20; Acts 4 v 27-28.**

- *So how should we think about our own circumstances—however difficult?*
- *And what is the most important thing that we should be living for—whatever our troubles?*

Paul is not even bothered about some people (who may or may not be genuine believers) who were preaching about Jesus for selfish reasons. **The most important thing is that people hear the good news about Jesus.**

time out

Christians are loved by the living God, who gave His Son for us. We are destined for heaven, and our message is unstoppable.

- *If you are not rejoicing, which of these have you forgotten about?*

pray thru'

Some of us are naturally optimists. Others will see their glass as "half empty". But all of us need to be filled with the conviction that God's message for the world is the most important thing of all—and it's unstoppable!

- Pray that you would see this clearly.
- And pray for an opportunity today to tell someone about our wonderful forgiving, gracious Saviour.

An impossible choice

Reading: Philippians 1 v 18b-26 **Friday** 28 January

28

One guaranteed way of killing a polite conversation is to bring up the subject of death...

Why do people in general not like to talk or think about death—their own or others'?

The joy of dying

Read v 18b-22

Who does Paul say he is being helped by?

Does Paul know what will happen to him?

What does he think about his own death?

Paul seems to have a sense that God may spare him this imprisonment, and he may be able to visit his Philippian friends once again. But he is supremely confident he will win! It will work out for his "deliverance" (literally: "salvation"). He has confidence in the sovereignty of God, that whatever happens it will be for the glory of Christ—whether he is released, remains in prison or is executed. But for now he is rejoicing in the sustaining power of God's Spirit, and the encouragement of his praying friends.

Have you grasped this truth yet? If you are in Christ, you are utterly, utterly secure. You are living and breathing at this moment so that you can bring glory to Christ. God has placed you where you are so that you can be a witness to His saving grace to those around you. And even death should hold no fear for you—rather, the opposite. It is not life's dead end. It is the gateway to eternal joy.

The joy of living

Read v 21-26

Explain to yourself what the words of v 21 actually mean.

What is the struggle that Paul is having in v 22-26?

Notice that Paul doesn't see his own life and death as being about himself. His concern and love is for his brothers and sisters in Philippi, and, no doubt, the rest of God's people. He knows that by living, he will have the opportunity to help, teach, encourage and guide them. But he also knows that how he endures his suffering and death will be a help and example to them as well. Death is better for him personally, but as a slave of Jesus (v 1), he wants to do His will now for the growth and joy of his friends.

We are not called to merely **be** Christians, or even to live **as** a Christian. Paul says: "to live **is** Christ..." The glory of Jesus is to be our foundation, our motive, our priority, our aim. The very reason and purpose of our existence the heartbeat of our lives.

Read v 21 again

Can you honestly say this is true for you? Talk to God about what you are living for today, and about how you feel about your own death.

Fight club

Reading: Philippians 1 v 27-28a **Saturday** 29 January

Confrontation. Most of us avoid it like the plague, and we're more than a little wary of people who seem to relish a fight...

Live for the gospel

Read v 27

What's the difference between fighting ***against*** *someone and fighting* ***for*** *something?*

How will Paul's instructions in this verse help them to contend in a godly way?

Whenever we are involved in a fight of any kind, there are dangers lurking on every side. We can over-react. We can demonise the opposition unfairly. We can find ourselves doing and saying things that we would not normally do. We easily become proud and defensive.

But Paul's first instruction is to live in a way that is worthy of the gospel. That gospel is all about God's generosity, grace, forgiveness and love towards hostile rebels like us. The way we live must show the same qualities—even, perhaps especially, to those who oppose us!

Fight for the gospel

Read v 27 again

What are the Philippian Christians to be fighting for or against?

How should they be contending?

We must contend for "the faith of the gospel"—the message of God's grace to us through Jesus' death. But there are two other hidden struggles implicit in this verse. There is the internal struggle we all face to remain godly. And there is the struggle we face to remain united as believers against our common enemy.

Which of these three battles do you find hardest to win?

The Christian faith is more like football than golf. We are not called to contend in isolation, as though we are individuals competing in a tournament. We are called to be united "as one"—to be a team. Sadly, Christian history reflects how much of a struggle this is for us.

Without fear

Read v 27-28a

Why do you think we should not be frightened of those who oppose us?

- **In Christ, we've already won!** The worst they can do is kill us, and all that will do is speed us on our way to the joy of being with Christ.
- **All things are in God's sovereign hand.** The only reason they have any power at all is because our loving Father allows it. Our Father knows what He is doing, and how He will work out this "problem" to the praise and glory of His Son, our Saviour.

God's actions: our response

30

Reading: Psalm 111 **Sunday** 30 January

This psalm pairs perfectly with the one that follows (wait until next Sunday!).

Psalm 111 recalls God's active goodness, and reminds us how to respond to Him. Then Psalm 112 tells us what life can be like when lived that way.

Read Psalm 111

Notice the opening command, and see that the writer is doing just that.

Fill in the table below with the reasons why the writer gives such praise to God.

What has God done?
What does God go on doing for His people?
What do God's deeds show about His character?

Given that God is like this, what is the right way to respond? Draw out your answer from v 2b, 4a, 5a and 10.

pray thru'

Read verse 10 again: *See what it means to be truly wise?*

- ***Since God is Creator and ruling Lord****—revere Him (10a).*
- ***Since God is awesomely holy and good****—obey Him (10b).*
- ***Since God is like this****—praise Him (10c).*

Go through your answers above, and turn each of them into expressions of reverence and praise. And ask for His help to be an obedient and thankful servant.

The gift of suffering

Reading: Philippians 1 v 27-30 **Monday** 31 January

The devil is against the gospel, so his people will always oppose those who stand up for it. Paul gives his friends—and us—three encouragements.

1. A sign

Read v 27-28

What is the sign (v 28)?

What is it a sign of?

When believers stand firmly together against gospel opposition, and without fearing their opponents, it is a sign that confirms the truth of the gospel. Normally, people would crumble and divide, or run away in terror, when they are opposed. But Christ's Spirit within His followers enables them to stand united and unafraid against even the most savage of opponents.

It's a sign that their faith is genuine, and also that their opponents' opposition to the gospel of God will mean judgment for them.

2. Suffering is a gift!

Read v 29

How does this verse completely change the way we think about suffering for the gospel?

The world can only see that suffering is bad, or as a curse from God that we must flee from at any and every opportunity. But Christians must see it differently. The very heart of our faith is the cross of Christ. It was suffering that seemed like a disaster to everyone at the time, but was the perfect plan of God to bring redemption to the world.

time out

Opposition is part of the deal when you become a Christian. But, remarkably, it is something we can rejoice in.

Ponder Matthew 5 v 10-12; 16 v 24.

pray thru'

This is difficult, I know. But if you are suffering for your faith, do you see it as God's loving gift to you? It sounds good in theory, but if you are facing the daily pressure of hostility from someone close to you, then it is a big ask. But then **Matthew 5 v 10-12** is a big promise from God to hold on to.

Ask God to show you how you are truly "blessed" by this gift.

3. Suffering is normal!

Read v 30

What do we tend to assume when things go wrong?

How does it help to know that Paul is going through it as well?

Paul, in prison, wants to encourage them to see that it is not unusual to suffer. We tend to assume, falsely, that we are alone, and that it is a sign of God's displeasure. Quite the opposite! We can take comfort in knowing that this gift is something that all God's people share in together.

Growing together

Reading: Philippians 2 v 1-4 **Tuesday** 1 February

When you become a real Christian, God changes you. We start to experience the truth of what it means to know God...

Signs of change

Read 2 v 1

What are the four signs that Paul points to in his reader's lives that show God is at work in them (clue: four "ifs")?

Genuine Christians will be strengthened by the thought that they are joined to Jesus; they will be more confident because they know that God loves them; they will start to sense a deep bond with other Christians; they will start to love other people in a new and different way. This is all the work of the Holy Spirit in our lives.

Obvious question: do you experience these things?

If not, what should you do about it?

Signs of growth

Read v 2-4

How does Paul want them to grow?

Paul wants them to think the same! To have the same mind, purpose and spirit. He wants us to think that Jesus is everything, that everyone must hear the gospel about Jesus. He wants us all to think that we are not important, but that other Christians are more important than us. Then we will be united and humble and loving—and living for Jesus together.

time out

Our culture encourages us to be proud to think differently from each other. But God's truth is one. We each have different personalities, different gifts, and a unique relationship with God. We will not become "Christian clones". But as we read the scriptures together, sit under sound teaching, and encourage each other, we will grow to have the same understanding of God's word, and what is important in life.

Signs of danger

Read v 3-4 again

What threatens to shipwreck this growth in our Christian lives?

Selfishness. The devil wants us to forget that Jesus has changed us. And our hearts are only too ready to be selfish and ambitious and proud.

In what ways does proud thinking show itself in our churches?

Pray that you, the congregation you are part of, and all of God's people will remember what they have been called to. Pray v 2 for yourself and other Christians you know.

Growing like Jesus

Reading: Philippians 2 v 5-11

Wednesday 2 February

Many of us have heroes of the faith that we try to emulate. People whose wisdom or love or thinking or maturity or zeal we aspire to. Paul wants us to focus primarily on the Lord Jesus…

Think like Jesus

Read v 5-11

What exactly was Jesus' attitude, that Paul says we should imitate?

Why do you think we find that so difficult?

The Lord Jesus was happy to be a servant, and He was glad to become nothing. He even embraced injustice, suffering and a horrible death, because He loved His Father, loved the world, and knew it was the only way to bring forgiveness to us.

pray thru'

Think for a moment about who these incredible verses are describing. Jesus is the Creator! All the angels of heaven worship and adore Him! All the forces of evil run screaming at the mention of His name! And yet He left the glory of heaven to come to the lowest place on earth. He exchanged riches for poverty; a sapphire-paved court for a stable floor. *Out of love for you!* It is a mark of His true greatness that He was so humble. dedicated, obedient, and selfless. And it is a mark of our utter weakness and sinfulness that we struggle so hard to be any of these things. So:

- *Time for some confession?*
- *And time for some praise?*

Act like Jesus

Read v 5-8 again

So will you be willing to do the worst jobs at church? Will you be happy not to get honour and respect from others?

And will you be delighted to put other people first? Will you not worry about piling up riches and possessions and glory for yourself, but look towards a future reward?

And if not, what does this show about you?

Give glory to Jesus

Read v 9-11 again

What did the Father do as a result of Jesus' humble service?

When someone risks their life to rescue a child, our culture rightly honours them. I read a news report today about a man who had died rescuing a drowning child. They had put up a plaque to commemorate his heroism, and his widow said that she "could not be more proud of him for what he did".

Jesus gave His life to rescue *all* His children from hell! And so the Father pours the greatest honours on Him, and exalts Him above everything else.

time out

One day everyone will see Jesus for who He really is. Everyone will honour Him when He returns in glory. Some willingly, others grudgingly. Make sure you are in the former category…

Salvation shines

Reading: Philippians 2 v 12-18 **Thursday** 3 February

You get the best Christmas present ever! A brand new, shiny, sporty car. But a month on from Christmas it is still in the driveway. Untouched; unused...

Working out!

Read v 12

- *I thought the gospel of God's forgiveness was free! What is it we have to work at?*
- *I thought the gospel of God's forgiveness was about being loved! Why must we work it out in "fear and trembling"?*

Just like the present of a brand new car, we have to put the gospel to work in our lives. It **is** free, but it requires us to engage our will and grow in obedience to it. And when we realise what this "free" gift cost our Lord and Saviour, it is never something that we can take lightly or for granted. It is a treasure we hold in fear and trembling—not because it might be taken away from us, or that, somehow, God has attached conditions to it—but because it is an enormous privilege to have been chosen to receive it.

Working in!

Read v 13

- *Why is this such an encouragement after v 12?*

God never leaves us to work on our own. He works with us and in us. He has a big plan for every Christian—to make us pure and holy like His Son Jesus. He will help us tell the truth, show love, control our anger, think pure thoughts, speak up for Jesus, be generous and humble.

pray thru'

Does this seem a million miles away from where you are in your life? The biggest problem for us is that we do not want to change to become like Jesus. But this is the very miracle that God will work in your heart:

- Dare you ask Him to work in your heart to change you? Ask Him now, knowing that it is a prayer He will answer.

Shining out!

Read v 14-18

- *What two things will shine as we work out the salvation that God has worked in us (v 15-16)?*
- *And what will be the character of our Christian lives—how will other people see us (17-18)?*

Our **lives** will be as different from those around us as stars shining against the blackness of the night sky. But we will also share the gospel **words** of salvation with others. There will be persecution, and yet there will also be a deep and unmovable joy and gladness, because of what God has done for us in Christ.

A life to live, words to speak, joy in your hearts. Which of these do you struggle to find most?

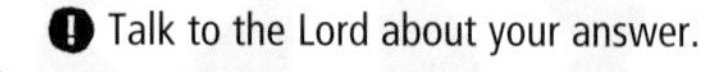

- Talk to the Lord about your answer.

A great example

Reading: Philippians 2 v 19-24 **Friday** 4 February

Have you ever been in the place where you have said to God: "Whatever You want me to do; wherever You want me to go—I will do it."

Jesus first

Read v 19-22

"I'm sorry, I can't help because..." What excuses do we make to ourselves, others, or God for why we are not able to help?

Some reasons are legitimate—we have other godly responsibilities to our family or others. But often, it is because we put **ourselves first.** If we offer to help on *that* camp, or commit ourselves to being at *that* meeting every week, or being responsible for *that* ministry, or meeting up regularly with *that* needy person, we will have to work hard, or miss out on something else we want to do.

Why was Timothy willing to go?

For Timothy, going to visit the Philippians meant a dangerous journey of perhaps 800 miles on foot and by boat. There are many reasons why he went. He loved the Philippians. He loved the Lord Jesus. He loved the gospel. And he also loved Paul, and wanted to serve and encourage him. All these things took precedence over his love of self.

What an example to us! You may not be as free of responsibilities as Timothy was, but will you pray that you will be like him? Willing to go and serve for Jesus' sake?

A trusted servant

Read v 22-24

How does Paul feel about delegating responsibility to Timothy? Why?

Paul knew he could trust him. Timothy had travelled with him on his journeys. They faced many dangers together as they told others about Jesus, and Timothy had already proven himself in many difficult jobs. But their relationship wasn't a "professional" one. In Christ, they worked as father and son—committed to one another. This little phrase points to the way we should serve as a younger Christian with older believers—respectfully as children in the faith. It also helps us see how older Christians should mentor and train those who are younger than us in the faith—giving responsibility and nurturing them as a father would his child.

Would you like to be a trusted servant of Jesus? Then think how you can begin...

Start with little things that no one else wants to do. When you say you will do something, be sure to do it. And always do it well, for the Lord Jesus. And seek out the help, advice and nurture of those who are older in the faith than you.

Talk to the Lord about your next step.

Another example

Reading: Philippians 2 v 25-30 **Saturday** 5 February

How do Christians learn to think and live right? By copying. Supremely, we copy Jesus, but we also copy Paul and Timothy as they live for Christ. Now Paul adds another example to the list…

Dear brother…

Read v 25-30

What do we learn about Epaphroditus from these verses. What kind of man was he?

How does Paul describe him?

The Philippian Christians had sent Epaphroditus to Paul to "take care of his needs"—to serve him. The Bible does not suggest he was a preacher, or that he had great gifts. He was homesick and anxious for the feelings of his friends in Philippi. **But look how Paul values him:** Brother! Fellow worker! Fellow soldier!

time out

We need to value each other in Christ! We are working together for the same Lord on the same mission. We all have different gifts, and different parts to play. But in Christ we are all equally valuable, and should therefore honour and value each other. **Read 1 Corinthians 12 v 21-27.**

And what an encouragement for "ordinary believers" like you and me! You do not need great gifts like Paul and Timothy to serve Christ. You can be young and not know much. You can be old and not able to do much. But in Christ you will always be valued, honoured and useful.

Ready to take risks

Read v 25-30 again

What happened to Epaphroditus?

Gospel work is dangerous. A friend of mine has almost died a number of times from illnesses he has caught while translating the Bible in Africa. But does that stop him going back? Never! And many early missionaries to Africa and Asia packed their belongings in coffins—knowing that they would most likely die taking the gospel message to those who were living in darkness.

Epaphroditus risked his life to encourage Paul in prison, and nearly died as a result. We should honour and respect those who will take such risks for Christ (v 29).

But we should also copy them. We may not have the opportunity to put our lives on the line for our Lord and Saviour, but should we not risk our reputation, our wealth, our time, our energy to support the work of the gospel?

A life less ordinary: part 1

Reading: Psalm 112 **Sunday** 6 February

This psalm is the other half of Psalm 111: it may not seem obvious at first, but read on...

Read Psalm 112

The rewards of godliness

Read v 1-9

Some of our most powerful yearnings are met by godly living:

- **Security: v 3, 6, 7.** Psychologists say that our most fundamental need is for security: financial, emotional and physical. Notice that, even though he's rich (v 3), it's not where the psalm writer puts his trust. That is firmly placed in God: so even the loss of his wealth will not shake him. In Christ, our riches are secure for ever: **see Ephesians 1 v 3**.
- **Significance: v 2, 9.** Held in respect by others, and by his family. In Old Testament times, there was a more physical understanding and bestowal of God's blessings, which is not ours to claim. But the truth remains that the godly among us are those who we should hold in highest honour, irrespective of our wealth or worldly status. **See James 2 v 1-5.**
- **Survival: v 2, 3, 6, 9.** Our greatest drive: to survive! Again, the Old Testament believers had but a shadowy understanding of life beyond the grave, so here his survival is expressed by promises of children and honour. But in Christ we can look with confidence to the resurrection: **see 1 Corinthians 15 v 51-57**.

Which of these "drives" do you think you are most driven by?

The wages of sin

Read v 10

See how all these three are taken away from those who choose wickedness rather than the way of the Lord! This is the lie and deceit of sin.

Even though the ungodly man is pursuing the same drives for security, significance and survival, he ends up empty handed: his longings "will come to nothing". And his self-consuming hatred of the righteous man is kindled when he sees that all the things he has longed for have been given by God to the one who trusts Him.

There really are only two ways to live. We either trust that God's way and God's provision are our only hope. Or else we listen to the devil's oldest lie—that rejecting God, and following our own desires will lead to our fulfilment. It's an old lie, but it still has a powerful influence upon us. Turn to the Lord in prayer now and ask for His help to believe in His way—and to live it.

Read Mark 8 v 34-38.

Positive faith

Reading: Philippians 3 v 1-7 **Monday** 7 February

Paul wants us to look for, and copy, good examples of people who live for Jesus. But he also wants us to watch out for bad examples too…

Sure—and wrong!

Read v 1-7. Then re-read v 4-6

What makes you sure that God will accept you?

What did previously Paul rely on, as a Jew?

When Paul was young, he was very sure of himself. He came from the best family; he knew the Bible back to front; he was disciplined in law keeping; he gave his whole life to God. **But he was utterly, completely wrong!** It's like he came out of the exam room, absolutely convinced he was going to get **A++**. But to his shock he discovered on the Damascus road that God had awarded him a big fat **F!**

apply

And what about you? Is this what you are relying on? Your lovely respectable family, perhaps with a fine Christian heritage? Or your morality and giving; or your involvement in church; or your Bible knowledge and your devoted prayers; or your experiences of feeling God's presence and singing His praises?

"F" says God. Worthless. Useless. These things make God sad, not happy. What **we do** will never get us to heaven.

Sure—and right!

Re-read v 1-3

What does Paul mean when he says that Christians are "the circumcision"?

What are the three marks of those who God is genuinely pleased with?

Paul wants the Philippians to be careful of some Jewish believers. They insisted that, in order to be acceptable to God, Gentiles must also follow all the Jewish laws, including circumcision—the ancient mark that someone belonged to God's people. He says that Christians are the true people of God (the true circumcision), even without having the physical sign on their bodies. Unlike people who trust in their religion, genuine believers will:

- **Worship by the Spirit of God:** they are able to worship and please God without the trappings of religious ritual or ceremony, because the Spirit of God lives in their lives (**see John 4 v 21-24**).
- **Put no confidence in the flesh:** we know that if we trust our own efforts, we will be lost forever. We know that our lives are an "F"!
- **Glory in Christ Jesus:** We know that Jesus has taken, and passed for us, the exam that we could only fail. He got 100%—and we adore him for it!

Is this what your faith looks like?

If it is, then you will want to respond to the apostle's encouragement in verse 1…

Knowing Jesus

Reading: Philippians 3 v 7-11 **Tuesday** 8 February

Here's a curious piece of gospel mathematics. ***Question:*** *If Paul loses everything—what does he have left?* ***Answer:*** *Everything!*

Everything is loss...

Read v 7-9

What are the things that Paul considers worthless (remind yourself by looking back at v 4-6)?

How does he now view them? Why (see v 9)?

Notice that he is not saying: "The Jewish law and life were good, but when the gospel came along, I realised it was better, so I left these other things behind". He is saying that he considers these things to be a load of rubbish! The whole way of thinking led him to be an *enemy* of Jesus, and trust in a system that could never deliver righteousness.

apply

Are you someone who has a "religious" background? If so, how do you look at that whole episode of your life? Do you have warm feelings for it, or do you recognise it for what it really is—a death trap that could never deliver where it truly counts.

...compared with knowing Christ

Read v 8-11

Paul says that he "knows Christ" (v 8), but also that he "wants to know Christ" (v 10). Why does he say both these things?

We say we "know someone" if we have met them, or been introduced to them. But when we are in a relationship with someone, we learn more about them as time goes on. This is the same with our life in Christ. If you are a Christian, you can say that you "know Christ". But you will want to spend your life (and eternity!) getting to know Him better.

But what particularly does Paul want to know about Jesus more intimately (v 10)?

Perhaps you want to know more about Jesus—His character and thoughts and passion. And perhaps you want to experience His resurrection power in your life. But what about knowing more intimately and deeply the "fellowship of sharing in his suffering, becoming more like him in his death"?

What do you think this means?

And where does this life of growing knowledge of the Lord Jesus lead (v 10)?

pray thru'

Jesus left glory to suffer and die, and be glorified in His resurrection (2 v 5-11). It must be the same for everyone who follows Him—everyone who is "in Christ". Resurrection glory only comes through the experience of suffering and service.

Talk to the Lord about how this thought makes you feel.

Run the race

Reading: Philippians 3 v 12-16 **Wednesday** 9 February

Paul is warning his friends about the danger of thinking that we can work to earn our forgiveness. But there are opposite dangers that needs to be addressed…

Read v 12-14

What are the dangers he is warning us about?

"I've already made it!" Sometimes Christians can been drawn into thinking that because our forgiveness is a gift, then we need do nothing more. They say "I'm already perfect—I don't need to do anything more".

What would Paul reply to this person?

"Jesus has done everything for us, so we must just sit and do nothing." I don't need to make any effort in the Christian life; I've just got to go with God's flow…

What would Paul say to this person?

Of course, there is truth in both these statements. In Christ, God treats us as if we are perfect. And it is *God's work* to sustain, equip and enable us to live for Him. But these truths should lead us to **action** as believers, not sloth! Because I am perfect in Christ, I will strive to become what I already am in Him—by fighting against my own sin. Because heaven is promised to me, I will push on to get there. The sign that God is at work *in* me, is that I am at work *for* Him. And He does not bypass my will in making that a reality.

How to run the race

Paul says that the Christian life is like a race that God has called us to take part in. The finishing line is ahead of us, and we are not to be distracted in our efforts to keep going and get there.

Read v 13-14

What does "forget the past" mean?

Our past can make us feel weak or that we are no good for God. If you have trusted Jesus, He has already forgiven all your sins and mistakes—even the horrific ones that you feel especially guilty about. We need to forget them, because God has already forgotten them! Jesus has taken all our sins away at the cross. **Read Isaiah 43 v 25.**

Read v 13-16

What does Paul want us to look forward to?

Some Christians have stopped running, but Paul knows he is not there yet. He sees the wonderful prize ahead of him—being with Jesus for ever. And he also knows that it takes us time to get our heads round these things as we grow to maturity. The main thing is to keep going (v 16)!

pray thru'

And this is not just a race—but a chase! Do you remember a time when Jesus first chased you, and took hold of you (v 12)? Now you belong to Him, He wants to bring you home. He calls you to chase after Him as you follow Him to glory.

Ask Him to help you forget the past, focus on the future, and follow Him.

Two ways to follow

41

Reading: Philippians 3 v 17 – 4 v 1 **Thursday** 10 February

Philippians is full of good examples to follow: Jesus, Paul, Timothy, Epaphroditus. Now he sums it all up by urging us to follow the right people...

The wrong people

Read v 17-19

Why is Paul weeping?

Many who seem like good people are, in fact, enemies of the cross. Like the people Paul mentions in 3 v 2, they are serious, dedicated, religious people. They may go to church—but they do not want to trust the Saviour who died for their sins. Their lives show they are not on Jesus' side.

What four things does Paul say about them in v 19?

time out

Does this seem harsh to you? Yet we know what our own hearts are like, and how good we are at putting on a respectable outward appearance when our motives are far from pure. If they remain enemies of Jesus, their destiny is hell. And they will take you with them if they can. **Beware!**

The right people

Read v 17, 19-21

What is on the mind of those who belong to Jesus Christ?

While most people go down the wide popular road that leads to hell, a few go along a narrow, difficult path that leads somewhere very different. Everyone else thinks we are strange, but this is what we are like:

- **We are citizens of heaven (v 20).** It's like we have a passport that says we were born in heaven. Our true home is heaven, but we must live on earth for a while.
- **We are waiting for Jesus (v 20).** Our glorious King is hidden for the time being, but we are anxiously waiting for His return, when everyone will see how wonderful He is (2 v 11).
- **We are waiting for Jesus to change us (v 21).** It's hard to be in pain, to be lonely, to be poor. But we will not be like this for long! Jesus will change our weak bodies, and make us like Him for ever!

There are only two kinds of people. Those whose lives are all about this world and themselves. And people whose lives are all about the world to come, and Jesus.

You can tell which one you are by the way you think and live...

Stand firm

Read 4 v 1

A young believer asks you: "How can I be a strong, growing Christian?" Look back over chapter 3 and sketch out the answer that Paul would give him.

Just do it!

Reading: Philippians 4 v 2-5

Friday 11 February

High-blown theory, or neat theology is never enough. How does this work in practice? Read on to find out…

The wrong people

Read v 2-3

What had these women done in the past?

How does Paul encourage them to make up?

What do you think it means to "agree in the Lord"?

Of course arguments burst out between people. Paul himself had been involved in fierce arguments with his brothers about things (**see Acts 15 v 36-40**). And of course none of us is perfect (3 v 12)!

What a tragedy that two loyal hard-working believers in this church renowned for its faith and love should quarrel. But notice how Paul deals with it. It is not just their problem. It is a problem for the whole church—this letter would have been read out publicly! They must sort it out with the help of their whole fellowship, not sweep it under the carpet, or allow it to fester unseen.

And they must "agree in the Lord" (v 2). There will always be healthy, legitimate differences between us on minor issues, and ways of doing things in church. But we must **never** allow these things to ruin our unity on the important things. We serve the same Lord, and have the same mission: to know Christ and make Him known.

time out

I have known churches utterly ruined by feuds between individuals that have gone on for years, unaddressed. What a disgrace to the gospel! If that is happening in your church, it is never just "their problem"—it is your problem too. Take a leaf from Paul's book:

- Don't ignore it. Don't take sides.
- Discuss it openly. Remind them, and everyone, of what unites us in Christ.
- Urge them to be genuinely reconciled, and to live the truths of **2 v 1-4**, and to follow the example of **2 v 5-11**.

Rejoice!

Read v 4

Why should we rejoice? How do we know that Paul is not being shallow about this?

He was writing from prison! There will be many things in life—illness, opposition, setbacks—that we will not rejoice in. But we can and should rejoice "in the Lord". Our forgiveness, our status as sons of God, our eternal home with Christ are never affected by circumstances—but we need to remind each other of these things regularly, or else the immediacy of our circumstances will turn our hearts to complaining and grumbling instead.

Be gentle!

Read v 5

We should always be kind and caring.

Why? Can you work out the connection in v 5?

How to wreck nervousness

Reading: Philippians 4 v 6-7

Saturday 12 February

More principles into practice from Paul, as he turns his attention to what we do with our worries…

Don't be anxious!

Read v 6

- *Can you command someone not to be anxious?*
- *What does Paul say we should do instead?*
- *How does that help?*

There is a horrible grinding noise as the plane lurches in the sky. You grip the arms of the seat. Faces are white and tense all around you. No one is looking at anyone. Then a calm, relaxed voice comes over the loudspeaker. "This is Captain Taylor speaking—absolutely nothing to be alarmed about." Then your friend turns to you and says: "I've heard about this guy; he's their most experienced captain, and a brilliant pilot—we're in safe hands!"

Simply saying "don't worry" often doesn't help someone who is anxious. We may be fretful because we feel under threat, or unsure about what will happen next, or think that things are out of control.

Paul's brilliant answer is—pray! Why? Because when we turn to God, we realise that no threat can harm His children; that He knows what is going to happen, and it will work out for His glory and your good; and that He is thoroughly and completely in control of things. It may not entirely take the knot out of your stomach, but it gives you the right perspective on what you are going through!

time out

- *What kind of things do you get worried about?*

Can you see how turning to God in prayer and praise and thanksgiving will help you get the right perspective on those things?

pray thru'

Pray now about those things. And don't just talk to your loving Father *about* them. Tell the Lord you trust Him to **look after** them. Ask Him to change your circumstances. But also ask Him to change your heart. Thank Him that He is in charge of all things, and that you are perfectly safe in His hands. And leave them with Him when you've finished!

Receive God's peace

Read v 7

- *What is the wonderful promise in this verse?*
- *What does worry do to our hearts and minds?*
- *How will God's peace guard us?*

It does not matter how bad things are. It does not matter how afraid you are. God's peace is much stronger. We cannot explain it; but knowing that the Sovereign God of the universe is on our side will protect us from giving in to bad feelings or wild, desperate thinking.

- *Have you experienced God's guarding peace in times of distress? If not, could it be because you have not taken the advice of v 6?*

Think right, do right

Reading: Philippians 4 v 8-9 **Sunday** 13 February

Think right

Many Christians believe that it does not matter much what they **think** about. The important thing is what they **do.** This is completely wrong, of course. Our mind matters because what we think makes us the people we are. Our thoughts and attitudes lead to our actions.

Read v 8

Weigh each of the words carefully. What specific things can you think of that fit each kind of thought that Paul is encouraging in us?

What are the opposites of each of these?

Which kind of bad thought do you find easiest to slip into? Can you work out why this is?

How does Paul suggest we deal with this?

time out

We can find it hard to fight wrong thoughts about sex or money. We have jealous thoughts, angry thoughts, selfish thoughts. Sometimes they just pop into our heads unbidden. We should expect to have unclean minds because our hearts are unclean. **Read Mark 7 v 21-23.**

So our strategy must be to fill our minds with good things and leave no room for these other things to filter in.

pray thru'

And notice who this list describes: Jesus! Go through each description, and think of something Jesus did or said that shows He is like that. And then adore your perfect, noble, lovely Saviour.

If we fill our minds with the world, then we will become like the world. If we fill our minds with Christ, we will become like Him.

Do right

Read v 9

What is Paul concerned to prevent happening in this verse?

What is the promise that is attached to it?

The apostle is concerned that we don't just **think right** in some kind of disconnected way, but that we actually put what we have learned into practice! Christian thinking is only valuable if it results in changed lives.

And what about you? You love to be at church to hear good teaching. You go to a Bible study perhaps and love to wrestle things through and understand them. You even read the Bible with *Explore* most days. Paul's challenge is this:

Is it making any difference to the way you live, and what you do day by day?

If God still seems far away, and your life still in turmoil, could it be that you are not enjoying the promise of v 9, because you are not obeying v 8?

How to be content

Reading: Philippians 4 v 10-13 **Monday** 14 February

As we'll see tomorrow, Paul was happy when Epaphroditus showed up from Philippi bringing a gift. But Paul was also happy before he came. Why?

The secret

Read v 10-13

*What reasons did Paul have to be unhappy with his situation (**see 1 v 13**)?*

What exactly is the secret of being content?

Paul had known both, and was now in prison with an uncertain future, separated from the friends he loved, and chained up. And yet he is content.

He has realised that living in plenty can be as miserable as living in want if you have not learned the secret of contentment, which is to know Christ and to be known by Him. If we depend on external circumstances for our contentment, then we will always be looking for more, and be disappointed when we don't get it. Christian contentment is *internal*. But not the self-generated contentment of the self-help books. It is trusting confidence in the God who supplies all our needs, and strengthens us to live for Him by the Holy Spirit working in our lives.

apply

So are you content inside? Have you discovered this secret for yourself? Or do you still believe that a nice house, or more money, or a better job, or a husband or a wife are the missing ingredients that will make you content?

And notice that Paul *learned* to be content. It didn't come easily, naturally, or immediately—it can take years. God wants to teach us this godly quality.

Are you on the path to learning contentment?

The strength to persevere

Read v 10-13 again

Does v 13 mean that Paul has the superhuman ability to do anything and everything?

We believe in a "prosperity gospel"! In Christ we are *so rich* that we do not consider it important to go chasing after the trinket treasures and pleasures of this world.

We also believe in a "power gospel". Not that God will enable us to fly or walk on water if only we believe enough. But that our Father will give us the miraculous strength to walk with joy and contentment through whatever life throws at us; and bring us home to His eternal kingdom safe and sound.

Read John 7 v 37-38.

We can enjoy the good and wonderful things that God has given us in this world. But we don't need any of them to be content or happy. You may not have money, houses, health or a spouse, but if you have Jesus, then you have forgiveness, peace and eternal life.

Giving to God

Reading: Philippians 4 v 14-23

Tuesday 15 February

Most Christians give only a little money to God. Paul loves the Philippians because they have given ***themselves*** *to God!*

Unusual giving

Read v 14-18

? *How does Paul describe their giving in v 14 and v 18?*

? *Can you see a pattern in these verses about how we should give to God?*

Their giving wasn't some mechanical obedience to a strict rule of tithing or such like. They gave to *share* in Paul's suffering; and they gave to *worship* the Lord in a way that was pleasing to Him. Their giving included sending Epaphroditus to Paul, and may have included food, books and other things, as well as their prayers.

The point is that their gifts of money were part of their partnership or fellowship with Paul in the work of the gospel. He was doing what they were committed to, and so of course they gave to support him.

apply

This is always where true Christian giving starts. Not with some arbitrary rule about percentages. They gave *themselves* first, and their desire to help Paul and share in the opportunity of his gospel preaching naturally followed.

? *So how do you see your giving? As a burdensome duty, or as a joyful privilege?*

time out

We can see a general pattern for Christian giving from these verses.

- They gave relationally—supporting Paul in many ways, not just with money.
- They gave together as a church.
- They gave generously, even when others were not.
- They gave consistently—supporting him in the bad times as well as the good.
- And they gave wanting to please God.

Giving safely

Read v 19-20

? *Does v 19 mean that Christians will never be poor? What does this promise mean?*

The promise is that God will supply our *needs* not our *wants*. Our Father knows what we really need, and will give it. So we can be generous without worrying about the consequences to ourselves. God will generously give us everything we need.

? *Do you truly believe that?*

Looking back

We've reached the end of this wonderful letter, so a brief pause to review:

? *What four examples does Paul want us to follow as Christians so we keep on the right path?*

? *What should our attitude be (2 v 1-5)?*

? *How will we stand firm as Christians (4 v 1)?*

? *How will we be joyful as Christians?*

Pray that these things would be true for you and the church you belong to.

1 CHRONICLES: Look back

Reading: 2 Chronicles 7 v 14 **Wednesday** 16 February

In 587 BC the Babylonians captured Jerusalem, destroyed the temple and forced the Jews into exile. Seventy years later the Babylonians were defeated by the Persians and some of the Jews returned to repopulate Jerusalem and rebuild the temple.

A credibility gap

But things are not as they had been promised for the returned exiles (**see Nehemiah 1 v 3**). Listen to how the prophets had spoken of the return from exile in Babylon and the restoration of God's kingdom:

Read Isaiah 40 v 1-5

Who will see the Lord's glory revealed when Jerusalem is restored (v 5)?

All God's people—and many more besides—would be gathered back to Jerusalem. *The problem was…* only a few actually returned and they were struggling.

Read Isaiah 9 v 6-7

What will mark the reign of David's successor?

God's enemies would be defeated and the son of David would reign over God's people in justice and peace. *The problem was…* the son of David was just a governor in a land ruled by foreigners.

Read Ezekiel 36 v 33-36

*How does Ezekiel's prophecy compare with the current situation (**see Nehemiah 5 v 3**)?*

The land would bloom like nothing since the Garden of Eden. *The problem was…* there were still famines in the land and the people were having to scratch a living.

What has gone wrong?

This is the context in which 1 and 2 Chronicles were written. The prophets Zechariah and Haggai responded to this "credibility gap" by promising an even bigger future. In the New Testament it becomes clear that God will gather people from all nations into a kingdom ruled by King Jesus in a new creation.

The Chronicler (the writer of 1 and 2 Chronicles) looks back to Israel's history and reinterprets it for the needs of his day.

- **1 and 2 Kings show what was wrong in Israel's history.** They show why Israel went into exile. They answer the questions: *"How could this happen? Has God failed?"* The answer is that it was Israel that failed and God has judged her.
- **1 and 2 Chronicles show what was right in Israel's history.** They answer the questions: *"Do we have a future? Has God given up on us?"* The answer is that, under King David, Israel had a glorious past and God has promised that David's line will always rule over God's people. Israel can have a glorious future.

Read 2 Chronicles 7 v 14

1 and 2 Chronicles is a call to turn back to God. It shows how Israel can restore the reign of God's king and the worship of God's temple.

Connected

Reading: 1 Chronicles 1 v 1 – 2 v 2 **Thursday** 17 February

Some people love lists. TV nights are devoted to the 100 best films, adverts etc. Websites tell us ten things we didn't know about someone. The Chronicler also loves lists.

Connected

Read 1 v 1-3

The Chronicler begins with a list of names. He begins right back at the beginning. He connects his readers with the first man, Adam. He wants to take us back to the Garden of Eden. As Adam's descendants we inherit Adam's call to know and serve God (**see Genesis 1 v 26-28**). As Adam's descendants we inherit Adam's sin and curse (**see Genesis 3 v 17-24**). And as Adam's descendants we inherit the promise that one of Adam's descendants will destroy Satan (**Genesis 3 v 15**).

- *We, too, are children of Adam. How should the calling of Adam, the sin of Adam and the promise to Adam shape our identity?*
- *What happens when we neglect one of these three truths about human beings?*

Chosen

Read 1 v 4 – 2 v 2

Throughout this list of names choices are being made. The Chronicler lists the descendants of each of Noah's sons (1 v 4-27), but then he picks out one family—the family of Abraham. He lists the descendants of Abraham's sons (1 v 28-34), but then he picks out the family of Isaac. He lists the descendants of Isaac's son Esau, but then in 2 v 1-2 he picks out Isaac's other son, Israel (= Jacob).

It's not the Chronicler making these choices. He's not picking his favourites. *It's God who is making these choices.* This is God's list. We share the curse of Adam. The choices in this list mark out the plotline of God's plan of salvation. They are moving us towards the descendant of Adam who will turn curse into blessing—Jesus. **See Luke 3 v 23 – 4 v 12**, where Luke connects Jesus to Adam and then shows how, unlike Adam, Jesus resisted the temptation of Satan.

Connected

Read 1 v 28

The Chronicler's readers are connected to Abraham and therefore to the promise made to Abraham: the promise of a vast people who will know God and live in a land of blessing.

Read Galatians 3 v 6-9 and 3 v 14.

- *Who are Abraham's true children?*
- *How are you connected to Abraham? What do you inherit?*

Hope in David's Son

Reading: 1 Chronicles 2 – 3

Friday 18 February

Read 2 v 1-2

God gave Israel his name (**Genesis 32 v 28**), but in Genesis he is usually known by his birth-name, "Jacob". The Chronicler uses "Israel" because that's what his descendants were called. Chapters 2 – 8 list the descendants of Israel.

The line of David

Read 2 v 3-4

After the reign of King Solomon, ten of the Israelite tribes rebelled against the rule of Solomon's son, Rehoboam. Only Judah and Benjamin, together with the Levites (the special priestly tribe), remained faithful to the line of David. In time the ten tribes were defeated and all but extinguished from history. So most of the Jews reading the Chronicler's history were from the tribes of Judah, Benjamin and Levi. As a result they get most attention and key positions at the beginning, middle and end. But it's more than a question of numbers...

time out

Look at 2 v 3 and 7.

What do these verses have in common?

These "asides" highlight the way sin brings judgment. These divine interventions within history point to the divine judgment at the end of history. The wages of sin is death (**Romans 6 v 23**).

Read 3 v 1-9

Why does the Chronicler give more space to Judah (2 v 3 – 4 v 23) than the other clans?

The reason Judah gets most attention quickly becomes apparent. Judah's line brings us to David (**see 2 v 15**). Judah matters because David matters.

The son of David

Read 3 v 10-24

And David matters because God promised that his descendants would always reign over Israel (**see 2 Samuel 7 v 12-16**). If God's people had any future at all, then this future must lie in a son of David. Their only hope was the restoration of the line of David.

Jehoiachin, the king at the time of exile, was a descendant of David. So maybe the Saviour would be one of his descendants? The Chronicler is doing with his lists what Isaiah does in his prophecy (**see Isaiah 9 v 6-7**)—promising a coming son of David who will save God's people and reign in peace.

time out

Look at Matthew 1 v 1-21.

Can you spot David? And Jehoiachin? (Matthew calls him "Jeconiah"). How does the angel describe Joseph in v 19? Jesus is the promised son of David—the One the Chronicler was looking for. He is the one who "will save His people from their sins" (v 21).

The prayer of Jabez

Reading: 1 Chronicles 4 v 1-23 **Saturday** 19 February

*In chapter 4 the Chronicler concludes his list of Judah's descendants (**compare v 1 and 21 with 2 v 3-4**). He focuses on Perez because this is David's line. But it includes someone with the name "Pain"—not an honourable name in such an honourable line!*

Named pain

Read verse 9

"Jabez" means "pain". The Chronicler wants to exalt the family line of David, but it has this glaring anomaly—a man called Pain. The reader might assume this person was a black mark in David's lineage—a sign that maybe this family could not be trusted. If you heard that someone's father had the nickname "Killer" you might think twice about trusting them. So the Chronicler is quick to highlight that, far from being the black sheep of the family, Jabez was actually *more* honourable. And Jabez did not get his name because of his character, but because his birth involved a painful labour for his mother.

time out

For the Chronicler it mattered that the line of David could be trusted and honoured. **Read Romans 1 v 1-4.**

Can we trust King Jesus? Why?

From pain to blessing

Read v 10

The prayer of Jabez has received a lot of attention in recent years. It has been singled out from all the prayers in the Bible as a model prayer that will bring blessing to those who pray it regularly.

- **What the prayer meant to Jabez.** Imagine a child today whose parents called them "Misery". It wouldn't be an auspicious start to life! And Jabez was part of a culture that put great store by the meaning of names. The name "Jabez" was like a curse. And so Jabez prays that God will turn his curse to blessing.
- **What the prayer meant to the Chronicler.** He writes to people in God's promised land, but that land is drastically reduced in size. They have experienced the pain of exile and now live under the threat of harm. The Chronicler writes to encourage people to turn back to God in prayer (**see 2 Chronicles 7 v 14**). If they do, then God will hear them as He heard Jabez.
- **What the prayer means to us.**

*What do **John 16 v 33** and **Revelation 21 v 1-4** say about being "free from pain"?*

Christians are not promised a life "free from pain" (quite the opposite, John 16 v 33). But the restoration after exile that the Chronicler prays for was a pointer to the life to come when we inherit a new earth and live with God "free from pain" (Revelation 21 v 1-4).

A life less ordinary: part 2

Reading: Psalm 112 **Sunday** 20 February

51

We're coming back to this psalm (looked at two weeks ago) to explore some more of its riches.

Read Psalm 112 again

Why it is called "godliness"!

It's an impressive picture of someone who has given themselves to God, and who is being richly blessed through, and because of that. But notice how this psalm exactly parallels the previous one! Compare v 3 in both psalms, and now compare v 4 in both psalms!

This man was like God! It's an outrageous claim to make, and yet the intention is clear: those who love God, and follow His word, will start to *become like God,* in His character, desires, hopes and priorities. And meditating on God's saving acts of mercy will lead to our becoming like Him in this and other respects.

time out

When someone asks: "What is God like?" we should be able to answer the question in (at least) two ways. Look at Jesus, the perfect Human who fully reflects God, and look at me—failing, struggling, but growing more like Him and the Father!

Read Hebrews 1 v 1-3; 1 Thessalonians 1 v 4-6.

What it comprises

We're to grow in righteousness—becoming like God—and we're given some practical examples of what this means in reality:

- a reverence for God (v 1)
- a delight in obeying Him (v 1)
- upright living (v 2)
- outgoing care for others (v 4)
- a don't-think-twice generosity (v 5, 9)
- acting with complete fairness (v 5)

Which one of these qualities do you need most help with now?

pray thru'

If life is good, we worry about the knock on the door, or the telephone call, or the visit to the doctor, or the item on the news that will bring our cosy lifestyle to a crashing halt.

But see verse 7. The man and woman of God will not think like that because they have a God who is sovereign over all things. His plan can never be frustrated—even the most devastating piece of news can never rock them, because they know and trust that God remains in the driving seat.

Is that true for you?—or do you need to ask the Lord for more faith and strength?

All Israel

Reading: 1 Chronicles 4 v 24 – 5 v 26 **Monday** 21 February

Among aristocracies, belonging to "a good family" is a way of maintaining the status of an elite few. It's a mark of who's "in" and who's "out". The Chronicler has focused on David's line and defended its honour. But he's not being exclusive. ***Read 9 v 1.*** *The Chronicler is concerned with "all Israel" (one of his favourite phrases).*

The unimportant tribe of Simeon

Read 4 v 24-31

Shimei's vast family is mentioned because it was the exception to the rule (v 27). The tribe of Simeon was not numerous and seems to have been absorbed into Judah by the reign of David (v 31). They never played an important part in Israel's history.

The easily-forgotten tribes across the Jordan

Read 5 v 18-19

The land of Israel is basically the area between the River Jordan and the Mediterranean Sea. But two and a half tribes—Reuben, Gad and half of Manasseh—chose to settle on the eastern side of the River Jordan. Being on the other side of the river meant they were easily forgotten.

Unimportant—but not to the Chronicler. *Easily forgotten*—but not by the Chronicler. The Chronicler is reminding us that the restoration of God's kingdom will not be complete until "all Israel" has been gathered in.

What does Paul understand "all Israel" to mean? **See Romans 11 v 25-27.**

The Chronicler is not just concerned about ethnic Israel. **Read 2 v 34 and 2 v 55.** Egyptians and Kenites have a place in God's kingdom. The good news is not just for all Israel, but for all nations—including nations we think are unimportant or we easily forget. Why not use a resource like *Operation World* (www.operationworld.org) to pray for some of the forgotten nations of the world?

The Chronicler weaves stories into his lists to show there is hope for all Israel. **Read 4 v 41-43 and 5 v 18-22.** The forgotten people had won an inheritance in God's kingdom in the past. And if they had done it in the past, then maybe they could do it in the future. The key thing was that the battle was God's (5 v 22).

Read 5 v 24-26

But when the people forgot about God, things went wrong. God judged them for their unfaithfulness. The future of God's people lies not in brave warriors, famous men or good families (v 24). It lies in faithfulness to God. It is the same today.

Is your hope for the church in brave warriors, famous men and good families—or is it in God?

The temple at the centre

Reading: 1 Chronicles 6 **Tuesday** 22 February

Levi at the centre

In the book of Deuteronomy, Moses said that the temple should be at the centre of Israel's life and worship. The Chronicler wants to restore this focus on the temple. And so the Chronicler puts the tribe of Levi at the centre of his genealogy because the Levites served in the temple.

Read v 64

In verses 54-81 the Chronicler lists the towns given to the Levites among all the other tribes. The Levites had no territory of their own because the focus of their work was the temple.

The priests at the centre

Read v 1 and v 16-19

Verses 16-19 start what we might think of as a standard genealogy for Levi. Three sons are mentioned and then each of their descendants in turn. But before the Chronicler does this he picks out the line of Kohath: **read v 1-3 and 10.**

Why does the Chronicler do this?

The line of Kohath is the line of Aaron. Aaron was the brother of Moses and the first high priest of Israel. This is the line of the high priests.

Atonement at the centre

Read v 48-49

The reason the temple, Levites and priests are so important now becomes clear. They offered sacrifices, "making atonement for Israel". Atonement in the Bible = dealing with our sin and God's judgment so we can be reconciled with God. At the heart of the life of God's people is atonement through sacrifice. It is the same today for us. The sacrifices of the Old Testament were pointers to the great and final sacrifice of atonement—the sacrifice of Jesus, the Lamb of God, on the cross. On the cross, Jesus was the High Priest making atonement *and* Jesus was the sacrifice.

What does it mean in practice for the atonement of Jesus to be at the heart of your life?

Read v 31-33

Throughout his work the Chronicler emphasises the role of music. In verses 31-47 he lists the temple musicians. Some people have even suggested he was a temple musician himself. The organisation of music for the corporate worship of God's people matters. It is a reminder to us of the importance of music in the worship of God. **See Ephesians 5 v 19 and Revelation 5 v 9.** At its best music helps us engage our hearts as we worship our God.

pray thru'

Pray for those who serve your church as musicians to help us praise God. Think of some songs that rejoice in the atonement Jesus makes for us through His death on the cross, and use them to express your praise to God.

Looking back, looking ahead

Reading: 1 Chronicles 7 v 1 – 9 v 34 **Wednesday** 23 February

In chapters 7-8 the Chronicler completes his list of the tribes of Israel. The section is full of contrasts between what Israel were and what they have become.

A mighty nation

Read 7 v 1-12, 40; 8 v 39

Israel was once a nation of mighty warriors. It takes us back to the glory days of David's reign (**see 2 Samuel 23 v 8-39**). There was a time when Israel was the superpower of the region. **Read 7 v 26.** The genealogy of Ephraim climaxes with Joshua because it was Joshua who led the people into the promised land.

When the Chronicler writes, Israel is no longer a mighty nation. It is a small province under Persian rule. But Israel's history is a reminder of what it once was. Perhaps a new Joshua might arise to give God's people victory over their enemies and lead them to a new home? It's no accident that "Joshua" is the Hebrew form of the name "Jesus"! Both mean "Saviour". Jesus is the Saviour who wins our inheritance in heaven.

A large nation

Read 9 v 1

The Chronicler has listed the tribes of Israel in some detail. This is a great nation with a long history. And yet... **Read 7 v 13.** The tribe of Naphtali only gets one verse in this genealogy. And there is one tribe missing altogether—the tribe of Dan. **Read 9 v 2-3.** Only people from four tribes plus some Levites returned to Jerusalem after the exile. The others were lost from history.

*This once great nation had been decimated. Why? (**See 9 v 1.**)*

The returned Jews were a long way from all God had promised. The restoration was far from complete. The Chronicler wants his readers to look for more. He wants them to look ahead with hope. But looking ahead requires looking back as well (hence all the genealogies). So, for example, in 9 v 22-23 the Chronicler links those who returned back to David and Samuel. The future for God's people will be found in the line of David, in turning back to God, in the atonement offered in the temple.

The Christian life is lived by looking ahead and looking back:

- ***Looking ahead*—read Colossians 3 v 1-4.** We look for an inheritance not in a land, but in a new heaven and earth into which our Joshua-Jesus will lead us.
- ***Looking back*—read Hebrews 2 v 17 – 3 v 1** . We look back to the sacrifice of atonement made by Jesus. This is the foundation of our hopes for the future.

Introducing King David

Reading: 1 Chronicles 9 v 35 – 10 v 14 **Thursday** 24 February

The Chronicler now changes gear. So far, he has covered hundreds of years through genealogies. Now he slows down and starts narrating the story of Israel's kings. 1 Chronicles 9 – 2 Chronicles 9 presents the reigns of David and Solomon as an ideal time. Hope for God's people will be found by living under the reign of God's king and worshipping God in His temple. But David was not Israel's first king...

King Saul

Read 9 v 35 – 10 v 12

1 Chronicles 10 is almost word for word the same as 1 Samuel 31. (The books of Samuel and Kings were the Chronicler's main historical sources.) The big difference is that 1 Chronicles 10 is *all* the Chronicler spends on Saul, whereas 1 Samuel spends 23 chapters on him (chapters 8 – 31).

Why do you think this is? (See Day 47, Feb 16 for the difference in approach between Kings and Chronicles.)

The Chronicler's account of Saul's life isn't even really an account of his life, but the account of his death. His burial at Jabesh (v 12) highlights the tragedy of Saul's life, for Jabesh had been the site of one of his great victories (**see 1 Samuel 11**).

What matters to the Chronicler is revealed in what he adds to the account in 1 Samuel:

Read 10 v 13-14

- **Saul ... was unfaithful to the Lord.** Unfaithfulness was how the Chronicler described the sin of Israel that had led to the exile (**see 9 v 1**). He keeps highlighting the link between unfaithfulness and judgment. This is both a warning and a hope. The Chronicler warns us not to be unfaithful to God, for faithlessness leads to judgment in this life or the next. But the Chronicler is also saying that turning back to God in faith leads to hope.

Part of Saul's crime was to seek guidance from a medium instead of seeking guidance from God.

Are there ways in which you live by the wisdom of the world instead of the wisdom of God?

- **The Lord ... turned the kingdom over to David.** For the Chronicler, Saul is simply the prelude to David. Indeed it has been said that for the Chronicler the whole of history from Adam (1 v 1) onwards is merely a prelude to King David.

The Chronicler looks back to David because he wants us to look forward to a coming King. And that coming King is Jesus. If the Chronicler were writing today, he would place Jesus at the centre of history. This isn't a quirk of the Chronicler. God's eternal plan has Christ as the centre and goal of history (**see Ephesians 1 v 3-10**).

King of all Israel

Reading: 1 Chronicles 11 v 1-8 **Friday** 25 February

Our writer is always true to history, but he is often selective. 2 Samuel 1 – 4 describes David's struggle to take the throne and be accepted by the people. The Chronicler leaves it all out. He goes straight to the point when the people acclaim David as king.

David the king

Read 11 v 1-3

The Chronicler emphasises that David was accepted by "all Israel". (He adds the phrase "all Israel" or "all the Israelites" (NIV) in v 1 and 4 to the material he uses from 2 Samuel.) The Chronicler wants to show the validity of David's kingship. But he also wants to show the people of God acknowledging David as king, because he wants his readers to acknowledge God's coming King. And the Chronicler wants to show that "all Israel" can be united by a common allegiance to the Davidic king.

We, too, must acknowledge David's son, Jesus, as our King.

In what areas of your life do you struggle to live in submission to Jesus as King? Use the words of 11 v 2 to acclaim Jesus as your Shepherd and King.

Is there a Christian you have fallen out with or find difficult to get on with? Your common allegiance to King Jesus is more significant than your differences. What could you do to restore your unity in Christ?

David the saviour

Read 11 v 4-8

God told the Israelites to drive the Jebusites out of the land (**see Deuteronomy 7 v 1**). But they had never succeeded until David. God's king is the saviour of God's people who fulfils God's promises.

From this time on Jerusalem takes on a special significance for God's people. It is the place where:

- **God is present with His people**, for this was where the temple was built.
- **God reigns over His people**, for this was the seat of the kings of David (v 7).

*What does Jerusalem point to? (**See Revelation 21 v 1-4 and 22-24.**)*

If you are a Christian today, you have so much to thank God for *now*, and so much to *look forward* to.

Spend some time thanking and praising Him.

A mighty God

57

Reading: 1 Chronicles 11 v 9 – 12 v 40

Saturday 26 February

In the fiction of Alexander Dumas, the three Musketeers together with d'Artagnan form an invincible band of warriors sworn to protect the king. Chapters 11 – 12 of 1 Chronicles have the same sort of feel (especially since they include "The Three").

Mighty men and a mighty God

Read 11 v 9-25

Chapters 11 – 12 list David's mighty men together with some of their exploits. These are stories of bravery, loyalty and heroism. They portray David as a mighty king with mighty warriors. The result is that David's reign extends over all the lands promised to Israel by God (v 10). But in all the stories of adventure we must not miss verse 9.

Why was David successful?

David was powerful because "the Lord Almighty was with him". We may never again see the likes of Jashobeam, Eleazar, "the Three", Abishai, Benaiah or "the Thirty". But the Lord Almighty is with us still.

time out

In **11 v 15-19** the Three go behind enemy lines to bring David water from Bethlehem. Pouring out blood was part of Israel's sacrificial system. David's action reflects this idea. The water the men bring is as precious as their blood, for that is what they have risked to get it. David is offering to God the offering they brought to him. But he is also showing that he *rules for Israel.* His concern is not to have water for himself, but to capture Bethlehem for God's people. He rules for the sake of his people just as Jesus does. **See Ephesians 1 v 22.**

Read 12 v 38-40. Chapter 12 continues the list of men who came to David's side at different times in his life. The point is again to emphasise that "all Israel" supported David as king (12 v 38). When God's people unite in obedience to God's king, the result is "joy in Israel" (v 40).

Read 12 v 16-18. The loyalty of the Benjamites is in doubt because Benjamin was Saul's tribe, and this was during the time when Saul was pursuing David (**see 12 v 1**). But to the Chronicler these words are a warning about what happens if people do not acknowledge the Davidic king. If people reject God's king, then God will judge them. In fact the Benjamites provide a model response to God's king in **12 v 18**.

pray thru'

Not all David's followers are Israelites. They include an Ammonite, a Hittite and a Moabite (**11 v 39, 41, 46**). In **Deuteronomy 23 v 3** no Ammonite or Moabite could be part of the Lord's assembly. But all those who acknowledge God's king are welcomed at His table.

Make **12 v 18** your song and prayer to King Jesus.

BIBLE IN A YEAR: **EXODUS 23-24 • 2 THESSALONIANS 2**

No equal!

Reading: Psalm 113 — **Sunday** 27 February

This psalm is the antidote to those who say: "It's true for you, but it's not true for me". I'm sure you've reached that point in conversation at least once. In effect they're saying: "Truth is relative, and I'm not interested in yours!"

Read Psalm 113

So wide

Read v 1-3

Of course this kind of relativism is not new. In Israel's day, every nation had it's own god—Dagon, Baal, Ashteroth, Molech to name but a few of those worshipped by the nations around Israel—and they were intimately linked with a nation's prowess in battle.

? *But what is different about the Lord, the God of Israel?*

? *What is the extent of His power, authority and control?*

? *What exactly are God's people called to do (v 1b, 2a, 3b)?*

time out

This is the mandate for the worldwide spread of the gospel. The God of Israel is the one true and living God. Jesus is Lord at the top of the Eiffel tower, at the headwaters of the Ganges, in a South African township and at a supermarket checkout. He is to be praised everywhere, because He is Lord everywhere...

Praising His Name means we are to rejoice, proclaim and celebrate His character: that is, what He is *like*, what He has *done*, who He *is*!

So high

Read v 4-6

He is even greater than the heavens, and has to bend down to inspect them! **Read Acts 17 v 22-34; 1 Samuel 5 v 1-4!**

Far below

Read v 7-9

? *See what this glorious, universe-encompassing God does.*

He takes care of the needy to rescue them (v 7), to transform them (v 8) and to satisfy their longings (v 9). Fantastic and awesome power is combined with intimate and personal care for His creation. No wonder the psalm ends as it does (v 9b)!

pray thru'

Spend some time praising God for His greatness. Think about how the Lord has dealt kindly with you and cared for others you know, and give thanks. In the time you have remaining:

- pray for those working overseas for the gospel
- pray for the needy, the poor and the childless that you know, that the Lord will comfort and raise them up.

JOHN: The great Provider

Reading: John 6 v 1-13 **Monday** 28 February

What good will it do you to be a Christian? John 6 tells us. Its theme is the benefits Jesus brings to those who believe in Him. The chapter begins with a "miraculous sign" (v 1-15) and ends with a long conversation in which Jesus brings out the meaning of the sign (what the sign signifies). Today we will look at the sign (v 1-13) and then tomorrow (v 14-15) at how people reacted to the sign.

The second Passover

Read v 1-4

Look back to **John 4 v 43, 54 and 5 v 1** to see where Jesus has been.

Where is Jesus now (6 v 1)?

"The far shore" means the opposite side to Capernaum; when Jesus crosses back, He is in Capernaum (see v 59).

"Tiberias" was a town on the shore of Lake Galilee founded about AD20 and named after a Roman emperor. The lake came to be known as "the Sea of Tiberias". This is one of many indications of John's eye-witness knowledge.

Why was the crowd following Jesus (v 2)?

From what we know about crowds and "signs" so far in John, do you think this is encouraging or not?

*What time of year is it (v 4)? Look back to **John 2 v 23** for what was happening a year before this.*

A hungry people

Read v 5-9

What simple point does John emphasise by the way he tells the story?

time out

Look carefully at verse 6.

What did Jesus know?

So why did He ask the question?

How does this help us understand the purpose of the whole miracle?

Jesus is trying to teach and train His disciples, so that they (and we) will learn from what He does.

A wonderful Provider

Read v 10-13

In each of verses 11, 12, and 13, John emphasises the *abundance* and *sufficiency* of Jesus' provision. Look carefully at the verses to see how he does this.

How do you think we ought to respond?

Tomorrow we will begin to think about the meaning of the miracle. But for now, take some time to think over the miracle itself. Think and pray about the depth and desperation of our spiritual hunger and the wonder of Jesus' abundant provision.

The Prophet-King

Reading: John 6 v 14-15

Tuesday 1 March

Today we listen to the responses of the people to the feeding of the 5000. From their responses we begin to learn the meaning of this "miraculous sign".

The Prophet

Read v 14

Now turn back to **Deuteronomy 18 v 15** (or v 15-20 if you have time). God promised a prophet like Moses. In a sense, all the true Old Testament prophets were like Moses; God spoke to them and then they told people faithfully what God had said. But this is not quite what God means in 18 v 15. Look at **Deuteronomy 34 v 10-12**.

- *What was it about Moses that had not been repeated—until Jesus came?*

Now think about echoes of Moses in the story of John 6 v 1-13:

- *Who led the Israelites at the time of the first Passover (v 4)?*
- *Who taught Israel from a mountain (Sinai)? Look at v 3.*
- *Who led Israel when God miraculously fed a huge crowd in the desert with "manna" or "bread from heaven" (Exodus 16)?*

Now we can see why they saw in Jesus a second Moses.

The King

Read v 15

- *If Jesus reminded them of Moses the rescuer from slavery in Egypt, why do you think they wanted to make Jesus a "king"? (Remember the role Moses had over Israel, even if he wasn't actually called a "king".)*

Think about the irony of forcing Jesus to be made king!

- *What sort of a "king" would He have been if He had agreed?*
- *Who would have defined what "kingship" meant?*
- *Why do you think Jesus withdrew and wouldn't let them do it?*

- *What sort of a king would you **like** Jesus to be? One who meets your felt needs?*

Think about the kinds of "Christianity" that offer us a Jesus who will meet our needs. What will it mean really to submit to Jesus, who is King on His own terms, and not "king" on our terms? Try to be practical and to think of areas where you need to let Jesus set the agenda for His kingship over your life, rather than you decide what He ought to do for you.

With Jesus in the boat

Reading: John 6 v 16-24 **Wednesday** 2 March

Remember the theme of chapter 6:
- what good will it do me to follow Jesus?
- what benefits will He bring?

In the dark without Jesus

Read v 16-17

This was the evening of the day when Jesus had fed the large crowd. Look back at verse 15 to see why the disciples get into the boat on their own. They are going from the NE side to the NW side of the Sea of Galilee (where Capernaum is).

What four things does John tell us about their journey in the second half of verse 17?

How do these combine to give not just a literal description but also a spiritual picture of their state?

time out

Have a look at **Mark 6 v 45-52**, which tells the same story (as does **Matthew 14 v 22-33**). Notice that Mark tells us this happened in "the fourth watch" of the night (between 3am and 6am). Since they started at nightfall, they had been rowing a long time but not very far!

Willing to take Jesus

Read v 18-21

*Why were they so frightened? (**Mark 6 v 49** tells us.)*

We know from Mark 6 that Jesus did get into the boat; but John puts it slightly differently in verse 21.

What does he say?

Notice the sequence: fear, reassurance, willingness.

Think about fear, reassurance, and willingness.

Why is it right to begin a relationship with Jesus by having a deep fear of Him?

Why should we be afraid?

Then think about reassurance.

How does the good news of Jesus reassure our fears?

Why does a proper willingness to receive Jesus only follow a proper fear and gospel reassurance?

"Immediately..." (v 21) may mean they miraculously got to their destination, or just that their arrival happened very soon after Jesus joined them. Either way, it is a picture of security with Him.

In search of Jesus

Read v 22-24

John tells us how the crowd gathered to hear the rest of the chapter. It is told simply and factually, as an eye-witness would. But notice the words, "in search of Jesus" (v 24). It's a theme in John's Gospel.

Food that lasts for life

Reading: John 6 v 24-33 **Thursday** 3 March

From verse 25 to the end of the chapter Jesus opens up the meaning of the feeding of the 5000. Remember the theme: what benefit does Jesus bring? And (today): how can I get that benefit?

Food that rots

Read v 24-27a

How many words about searching, looking for, and finding can you see in v 24, 25 and 26?

They were looking for Jesus; it all seems so worthy! So why is Jesus not impressed? They had not *really* seen "miraculous signs". Hey, but this was the crowd who had been there when Jesus fed the 5000! If anyone had "seen" the sign, it was them, wasn't it? So what was their problem? They were "working" and "seeking" pretty hard; the memory of full tummies saw to that. They wanted full tummies again.

But according to Jesus, what were they working for (v 27a)?

Food that lasts

Read v 27-29

Why can Jesus (and Jesus alone) give "food that endures to eternal life" (that is, inner food that gives a person a living relationship with God now and forever)? Look at the end of v 27.

In verse 28 they are still puzzled: "But what must we *do*?" they ask. Jesus had told them to "work" for eternal life food; so what kind of "work" does this involve? In verse 29 Jesus answers that it is one "work" (singular); there is only one thing we must do—and that is, not to *do* anything, but to *believe* in Jesus!

Food for life

Read v 30-33

Hear the irony: they ask for a "miraculous sign" like the manna in the wilderness.

But what have they just had (v 1-15)?!

Jesus explains that the manna wasn't the real deal; it was just a signpost to the real Bread, who is now there in the middle of them. See in verse 33 how the Bread is a Person! So what does He mean? Are we going to have to eat Him?! We shall see...

pray thru'

What kind of "food" are you seeking? And where are you going to find it?

Talk to the "true bread from heaven" about your answers.

The bread of life

Reading: John 6 v 32-40 **Friday** 4 March

Here is the first of the seven "I am" sayings of Jesus: "I am the bread of life." The passage helps us understand what He means.

Material hopes

Read v 32-33 and then v 34-36

The great feeding (v 1-15) reminds them of Moses giving manna in the wilderness. Verse 34 sounds good, but look at verse 36.

What do they still want from Jesus?

It's very like the woman in **John 4 v 15**.

Life: the real thing

Verse 33 helps us understand what "bread of life" means. It's shorthand for "gives life to the world." So "bread of life" means "bread that gives life or keeps alive".

Look carefully at v 35

To "come to" Jesus and to "believe in" Jesus are the same. Notice that this "bread" deals with both hunger and thirst; it is a picture of all we need to keep us alive. This is not so much about how we feel (whether we feel close to God, for example) as about actually being alive. And that means being in fellowship with the Father and the Son, as we shall see.

What the Father wants

Read v 37-40

Who comes to Jesus (v 37)?

If you are a Christian, it is because the Father decided in His love to give you to Jesus! This is a deep truth. Yes, you "looked" to Jesus in trust (v 40), like the Israelites looking at the bronze serpent (**John 3 v 14-15**); but you only looked to Jesus because the Father gave you to Jesus.

But what happens to those the Father gives to Jesus? What does Jesus say?

How safe are real Christians? Why?

In verse 37 He says He will never "drive away"—neither when we first come to Him in faith, nor ever afterwards. In verse 38 Jesus reminds us that He came to do just what the Father wants. And what does the Father want? Verses 39-40 spell it out.

Look up to the Father and praise Him for giving you to Jesus.

Look to Jesus and thank Him that He will never let you go.

Rejoice in this security for ever.

Grumbling

Reading: John 6 v 41-51 **Saturday** 5 March

Have you grumbled about food? Despite the "manna", the Israelites often grumbled in the desert.

Grumbling about Jesus

Read v 41-43

- *Why did they grumble?*
- *What did they know (or think they knew) about Jesus?*
- *Why did they assume this was all there was to know about Him? (What didn't they know, about Joseph, Mary, and Jesus' conception, for example?)*

There was more to Jesus than met the eye. You could "see" Jesus without really "seeing" Him at all.

It's easy to think of Jesus just in human terms.

- *How can you guard against reading the Gospel stories as if they were just about an unusual human being?*

Look back at **John 1 v 1-2**. This "Word" is the One we are reading about!

Listening to God

Read v 44-46

- *Who can come to Jesus (verse 44)?*

Verse 45 is probably from **Isaiah 54 v 13**, a prophecy that one day people will really listen to God.

- *Whenever someone really listens to God, what do they do (v 45-46)?*

time out

People often speak about "spirituality" in a vague way, as if all sorts of people "listen to God", without necessarily being Christian.

- *How would you answer someone who says he or she "listens to God" and yet doesn't come to Jesus?*

Food that lasts

Read v 47-51

- *What happened to the Israelites who ate manna in the desert?*
- *What is the difference with the bread Jesus offers?*

What extraordinary thing does Jesus say at the end of verse 51? It's not just that Jesus is the bread of life; it is the *dead* Jesus, who gives His flesh for the life of the world. This is such a surprise that it leads to a big argument, as we shall see tomorrow.

Take a few minutes to pray about your death. It's not morbid to do that. You don't know when you will die, whether young or old, suddenly or gradually. But—unless Jesus returns first—you *will* die. Pray about it in the light of the wonderful promise of Jesus in this passage. And let your thoughts turn to praise and wonder!

Hard rock

Reading: Psalm 114

Sunday 6 March

Psalm 113 asked us to consider "who is like the LORD our God?" This song gives a great illustration of why God is so unique: it points us to the definitive saving acts of God for His Old Testament people.

Read Psalm 114

Note that Judah, Israel and Jacob are all different names for God's people. It's a feature of Hebrew poetry that the same thought is repeated using different words.

Rescuer

Read v 1-4

What events is the psalm looking back on (v 1)?

What else is referred to (v 3-4)?

What remarkable event was all this leading up to (v 2)?

In the exodus (**see Exodus chapter 14**) God brought His people through the Red Sea (which "fled" at His command), and He later brought them into the promised land by a similar act of dividing the waters of the Jordan (**see Joshua chapter 3**).

pray thru'

Think of what it took to achieve this: the manoeuvring of the nations, the command of His creation, which (v 4) was delighted to obey Him.

Express your praise to God for His greatness!

Rule

Read v 5-6

What are verses 5-6 telling us about God?

Reverence

Read v 7-8

What is the only fitting response to God (v 7)? Why?

This all-powerful God shares His presence with His people (v 2), dwelling among them. But there's no place for treating Him casually or dismissing Him. **Read Hebrews 12 v 28-29**—and see how God uses His power (v 8)!

Amazingly, this awesome ruler of the nations delights in providing for His people: for the story behind verse 8 see **Exodus 17 v 1-7**.

We now look back on what God has done for us in Christ. God now brings so many benefits—rescue from sin, a future with those in His presence—to those who trust in Jesus.

Read Ephesians 1 v 3-14.

Feeding on Jesus

Reading: John 6 v 52-59 **Monday** 7 March

Today we come to the end of the "I am the bread of life" teaching.

A sharp argument

At the end of Saturday's reading Jesus said something puzzling. **Look back at verse 51.** What is the "bread"? No wonder they were puzzled!

Read v 52

Presumably they weren't so stupid as to think Jesus was encouraging cannibalism! The sharp argument was because they disagreed as to exactly what He meant by the metaphor. And how could "this man" ("this fellow") make this strange offer?

Taking life inside us

Read v 53-59

How many times does Jesus mention "life" or "live"?

This is the theme.

What does Jesus mean by eating His "flesh" and drinking His "blood"?

Flesh and blood spoken of separately like this point to *death*; this is looking forward to the death of Jesus.

time out

Is Jesus talking about the Lord's Supper/Holy Communion? No. These sacraments hadn't yet been given by Jesus, so no one listening could possibly have thought He meant that. This is a vivid picture of taking the benefits of Jesus' death inside us spiritually by faith. Having said that, this does help us to understand what the Lord's Supper means: *"John 6 is not about the Lord's Supper; rather, the Lord's Supper is about what is described in John 6."* (D.A.Carson).

Notice that receiving the benefits of Jesus' death inside us by faith...

(a) is essential—look at verse 53. The only real life available to human beings is because Jesus died.

(b) gives life now that will lead to resurrection later—notice the time sequence in verse 54. The Christian has eternal life now, and will be raised from the dead later.

(c) brings us into fellowship with Jesus—notice the word "remains" (or "abides") in verse 56. The only way really to live with Jesus is to trust His death.

(d) brings life that comes all the way from God the Father right into our hearts—read verse 57.

pray thru'

Thank Jesus for dying for you, and feed on Him in your heart by faith. Praise Him for the eternal life that He gives.

Desertion and betrayal

Reading: John 6 v 60-71 — **Tuesday** 8 March

The chapter ends on a downbeat note.

Hard saying or hard hearts?

Remind yourself of v 53-58 and then read v 60

Why did they call it "a hard saying"?

It wasn't really so hard to understand as a metaphor for taking the life of Jesus into us through His death for us. But it was hard to accept that Jesus' death should be the *only* way to get real life. It is just as hard today. The hardness was in their hearts, not in Jesus' saying.

Who can come to Jesus?

In verse 60 they asked: "Who can accept it?" It's a good question.

Read v 61-63

Only the Spirit can give life; and He does it through the words Jesus spoke. These are spiritual truths and only people in whom the Spirit works can grasp and accept them. Men and women by nature just don't and won't get it. It has always been like this, and it still is.

Now read v 65 and 66

Is Jesus surprised that some of His disciples are not really believers?

What has He taught them, that should help them understand what is now happening, with desertions and betrayal?

The words of eternal life

Read v 66-71

It's a poignant scene. Imagine the crowd of "disciples" evaporating as people peeled away and slipped off home.

What does Jesus ask the Twelve (the apostles)?

How does Peter reply?

How does Peter's reply link back to what Jesus has said in v 63?

What has Peter begun to grasp?

But the chapter ends (v 70-71) on a very sad note. Jesus *knows*. He is not taken by surprise.

Do you know people who were "Christians" but now aren't? Does this mean they were never Christians? Maybe, and maybe not! If they were Christians, then in the future at some point they will come back to following Jesus. But the sad truth from this passage is that it is possible for someone to follow Jesus when there's a big crowd and it's easy, but slip away when it becomes more challenging. Pray that you won't be like that.

Unbelieving campaign team

Reading: John 7 v 1-5 **Wednesday** 9 March

68

Every political candidate has a campaign team, who gets the candidate's name known and makes sure they have an impressive public profile. Except Jesus. Why?

First, **read through the whole of v 1-13** looking for words like "publicly", "in private", "in secret", "show", "see". This passage (which we will finish tomorrow) hinges on the tension between publicity and privacy.

Judea and Galilee

Read v 1

What is the difference (for Jesus) between Judea (centred on Jerusalem) and Galilee?

Look back at **chapter 5**, the last time Jesus was in Jerusalem (and especially **5 v 16, 18**). And look back to **6 v 15** to remember what just happened in Galilee.

time out

The most bitter hostility to Jesus came from the most religious people. Can you think of examples where real Christians have had a hard time from people who call themselves church people?

Show yourself to the world

Read v 2-5

The Feast of Tabernacles was in September/October so about 6 months have passed since the Passover Jesus spent in Galilee (6 v 3). Tabernacles was perhaps the most important feast of the year, so it would be a natural time to go to Jerusalem to make a splash in the newspapers.

Why do you think Jesus' brothers don't consider Galilee is good enough, and that doing things in Galilee might as well be "in secret"?

It's not that Jesus' signs in Galilee were done behind closed doors, but that it was a remote place, not really "where it's at".

What do you make of verse 5?

It's a surprise. It looks as if His brothers are His loyal campaign team—so why do you think their attitude shows their *un*belief?

The question is: who is in charge? Are they managing Him, or is He calling the shots?

pray thru'

In your prayer life, do you want to organise Jesus so that He does what you want Him to do? Pray that your prayer life will be turned upside down so that you really submit to Him and His timings.

Hide and seek

Reading: John 7 v 6-13

Thursday 10 March

We saw yesterday that the theme of verses 1-13 is whether Jesus will be public or secret. His brothers wanted to organise Him to be public. They imagined they were His campaign managers. But Jesus would not be managed by anyone except His Father.

The right time

Read what Jesus says in v 6-9

Why won't the world hate Jesus' unbelieving brothers?

The world loves those who belong to it. When Jesus says: "For you any time is right" (v 6), He may mean that they are not yet under the governing purpose of a loving Father; their lives drift along meaninglessly.

Who decides "the right time" for Jesus to make Himself public? (Not His brothers!)

Why does "the world" (human beings living without God and against God) hate Jesus?

How do we and others react when someone shows us up as wrong?

It's a litmus test. If we are angry and hate them, it's proof that we belong to the world. Pray for humility to respond to Jesus' convicting power with repentance.

Where is that man?

Read v 10-13

Jesus goes up to the Feast late and quietly, not with the big pilgrim caravan.

What three groups do we meet in Jerusalem and what do they want with Jesus or think about Him? Look first for the two mentions of "the Jews" (the Jewish leaders). Why do they want to find Jesus (see verse 1)? Then look at the two groups in the crowds.

Was it easy to say, "Jesus is a good man"? Is it any easier now to tell people publicly about the sheer beauty and goodness of Jesus?

time out

What will happen when Jesus makes Himself publicly known in the world, as the story continues? Will it be adulation, praise, being mobbed by His fan club? Or not? Why?

And what will it mean to be a loyal disciple of Jesus, then and now?

Think about this and pray for strength to stand with Him in a hostile world.

The key to knowledge

Reading: John 7 v 14-19

Friday 11 March

"The light shines in the darkness, but the darkness has not understood [= grasped] it" (John 1 v 5). From 7 v 14 through to the end of chapter 8, Jesus is in the temple—the light in the midst of the darkness.

Why is Jesus such a good teacher?

Read v 14-15

The feast of Tabernacles lasted seven or eight days. Jesus arrives midweek.

- *Why are the Jewish leaders so surprised when they hear Jesus teach?*

The word "learning" means a proper rabbi's education. "But He hasn't been through the system, or done the proper exams!" they say. It's a wonderful irony: they are surprised when the eternal "Word" (John 1 v 1-2), from whom all language, meaning and learning come, can understand and teach the Bible!

Now read v 16

- *How does Jesus answer? Why is His teaching so good?*

But is it true?

Read v 17

Jesus answers the obvious question: how can we *know* your teaching comes from God, who sent you? Are you surprised by His answer? It's not what we might have expected. To "choose" to do God's will means a whole direction of life lined up with really wanting to act the way God wants.

- *Why do you think only a life lined up with God's will can really understand the authority of Jesus' teaching?*

Verse 18 helps us understand

- *What does it teach about Jesus' motives?* Why *did He teach?*

It's to do with motives. Jesus' motives were not for His own glory. That's how we can know He is true. It will be the same with us. If our motives are for God's will, then we'll recognise the truth of Jesus' teaching.

Read v 19

- *How does this verse expose their bad motives?*
- *What does the law of Moses say about trying to kill an innocent person?!*

This proves they don't really want to do God's will.

Do you want to gain honour for yourself, for people to like you, think well of you, praise you? Of course you do! But that is what makes us "false" people (v 18). Ask God to search your heart and purify your motives.

Religion and reality

Reading: John 7 v 20-24 **Saturday** 12 March

In the temple there were all sorts of people. When John talks of "the Jews", he usually means the leaders. All the people there were Jews, of course. In yesterday's passage Jesus has been speaking to "the Jews" (see v 15) and accuses them of trying to kill Him (which they are).

Read v 20

Who is now speaking?

Perhaps these were pilgrims from outside Jerusalem. Either they don't know of the plot to kill Jesus or they pretend not to know.

The wrong astonishment

Read v 21

The "one miracle" is the healing of the sick man in John 5 v 1-10, the last time Jesus was in Jerusalem. What "astonished" them? Look back at **John 5 v 9, 10, 16**. It wasn't the healing!

The meaning of circumcision

Read v 22

Moses gave them the Sabbath (the 4th commandment—**see Exodus 20 v 8-11**). But circumcision actually came long before Moses; God told Abraham (the first "patriarch") to do that in **Genesis 17 v 9-14**. Every baby boy had to be circumcised on the 8th day of their life. So if a boy was born on Saturday, he had to be circumcised the next Saturday. They were quite happy to do that, even though it was a Sabbath.

Now think carefully about v 23

What is the connection between cutting off the foreskin of a baby boy and "healing the ***whole*** *man"?*

If it's ok to do the little symbolic healing, it's even more ok to do the complete healing, says Jesus. Circumcision was an outward sign of being right with God and therefore "whole" or "healed". But it was only the sign. How much better the reality Jesus brings!

Read v 24

"Appearances" means externals, such as circumcision, outward religious stuff. "Right judgment" is about reality, a life changed on the inside by Jesus.

pray thru'

Are there ways in which external religious things impress you more than a changed heart and life? For example, how much does it matter to you the exact way in which things happen in church? And how much does it matter to live a daily life of repentance and trust in Jesus, deep on the inside?

Whose glory?

Reading: Psalm 115 **Sunday** 13 March

Here's a song for those of you who want to put God first in every way.

Read it!

Not me

Read v 1

Silly, isn't it really, how we not only like to bask in the reflected glory of another, but also start to claim bits of it for ourselves. Whether it's something we've done—given a talk, served the coffee or organised the event—or someone we're involved with, pride whispers in our ear that we should accept the accolades for ourselves.

But any excuses we have evaporate next to the glory of the one who gave the gifts, the energy and even the desire to do it! The glory belongs to God and no other. **Read Isaiah 42 v 8; 1 Corinthians 4 v 6-7.**

Not them

Read v 2-8

Write a list from these verses of all the differences between the so-called "gods" and the living God.

Idols are God substitutes—pocket gods that we can control—whereas, the living God (v 3) does as He pleases.

Why is it ultimately stupid to trust this kind of "god"? (v 8)

time out

Some of our modern "gods" are obvious: cars, careers, family. Others, and perhaps the most destructive, are subtle and hidden. So give some time to working out what you really worship: your looks, your popularity, your status with others, perhaps?

Now reason with yourself: do they really give you what you want and need? And where does their worship ultimately lead? Ask God to help you smash them.

But Him

Read v 9-15

List the great reasons why the Lord is worthy of our worship...

And now

Read v 16-18

A great privilege and responsibility (v 16) is ours, and (v 17-18) just one lifetime to spend in His praise and service (not ours!).

In fact, the opportunity to praise God starts the moment you finish reading this sentence...

Is Jesus the Christ?

Reading: John 7 v 25-36 **Monday** 14 March

"Christ" is a title not a surname. The Hebrew is "Messiah"; it means, "the King anointed (or crowned) by God". Here's the big question: "Is Jesus the Christ?"

Where Jesus comes from

Read v 25-27

Here's the gossip among the locals ("the people of Jerusalem").

What do they think they "know"?

Look back at **John 6 v 42**. The irony is that they don't really "know" as much as they think they "know"!

Although some Jews were confident the Messiah would come from Bethlehem (see v 42), others thought the Messiah would suddenly and unexpectedly come into His temple (like **Malachi 3 v 1**), as a previously "unknown" man.

Now read v 28-29

Jesus "cried out", a loud announcement. "Yes, you know me, and you know where I am from" is ironic—"Oh, you really think you know who I am and where I'm from, do you? Think again!"

What does Jesus say about "knowing" the Father?

If we don't know the Father, we won't know (that is, recognise) Jesus.

The reactions Jesus provokes

Read v 30-32

How did people react to Jesus?

Why didn't anyone arrest Him—yet?

"His time" is literally "His hour", the time when He would voluntarily give Himself up to be killed. Who's in control? Jesus is!

Where Jesus is going

Read v 33-34

Who is Jesus going to?

Think about v 34. Why is it such a serious verse? Why is there nothing worse in eternity than not being able to go where Jesus has gone?

Notice how His words are repeated in verse 36.

pray thru'

Pray for non-Christian friends. Unless they turn to Jesus, the day will come when they will "seek" to go where He is, and not be able to. Pray they will turn to Jesus while there is time.

Read v 35-36

There was a large Jewish "*diaspora*" (dispersion) living outside Judea. "The Greeks" here means Gentiles, the rest of the world. There's a double meaning. Jesus would not go to the Gentiles yet; but after His resurrection He would go to the rest of the world through His apostles in the power of His Spirit.

Living water of the Spirit

Reading: John 7 v 37-44 **Tuesday** 15 March

Chapter 7 has been focused on the Feast of Tabernacles. Maybe a million people would be in Jerusalem.

Wonderful Jesus, life-giving Spirit

Read the start of v 37

How does John make clear that what comes next is very, very important? He says two things about the timing and two things about Jesus.

Read what Jesus says in v 37-38

- *Who is invited?*
- *What are they invited to do?*
- *And what are they promised?*

We might expect them to be promised personal satisfaction; instead Jesus says they themselves become sources of life to others. Real Christianity is a river (where the water flows on out), not a pond (where the water gets stuck).

Now read John's explanation in v 39

This is what Jesus meant when He offered the Samaritan woman "living water" in chapter 4.

- *What do you think John means by saying: "the Spirit had not been* given*"?*

The Spirit is eternal and He had been active since creation. But He was not given to live in all believers for ever until after Jesus died for our sins.

time out

Look back at how John gradually introduces the ministry of the Holy Spirit. Trace this theme through **John 1 v 32-33; 3 v 3-8; 4 v 13-14; 6 v 63**.

- *What do we learn about the connection between the Spirit and Jesus?*
- *And about what the Holy Spirit does for us and in us?*

Who is Jesus?

Read v 40-44

The claim to give the life-giving Spirit of God to people is astonishing. No wonder it led to a fresh bout of speculation. Is Jesus "the Prophet" (of **Deuteronomy 18 v 15**, also spoken of in **John 1 v 21**)? Is He "the Christ"? But then He ought to be from Bethlehem (**Micah 5 v 2**). Ah, but He is—if only they knew the history of His birth!

Thank God that if you believe in Jesus, He has given you the personal, eternal Spirit of God to live in your heart for ever, and make you someone through whom the life of God flows out to others. Pray that this wonderful outflow will happen more and more from your life.

No one ever spoke like this

Reading: John 7 v 45-52 **Wednesday** 16 March

Look back at John 7 v 1, 13, 19, 25, 30, 32 and 44.

What a theme of bitter hostility! And yet Jesus is still free, because His hour has not yet come. Today we see three responses to Jesus.

Amazement—the arrest party

Read v 45-46

What reason do they give for failing to arrest Jesus?

What has Jesus said since the arrest party were sent out in v 32?

Look especially at verses 37-39. No man had ever promised to give the Spirit of God to people before!

Hostility—the Pharisees

Not everyone was so impressed with Jesus' teaching.

Look back at v 12; then read v 47-49

What evidence do the Pharisees offer that Jesus is a deceiver?

Notice it is not about what He says, but about the kinds of people who believe Him. They're the wrong kind of people—ordinary, unprivileged people, not very well educated, struggling with life, bottom-of-the-heap people. The Pharisees despised them as a "mob".

Why do you think the Pharisees said there is "a curse" on the mob, who don't know the law of Moses?

Look at **Deuteronomy 28 v 15**. The Pharisees thought the only way to get God's blessing was to be very careful to keep all the detailed laws.

Courage—Nicodemus

Read v 50-52

What two things does John tell us about Nicodemus (v 50)?

One is a reminder of **John 3 v 1-15**. The other—with wonderful irony—says he was "one of their own number". So what is the true answer to: "Has any of the rulers or of the Pharisees believed in Him?" Actually it's not 100% clear whether Nicodemus really believes just yet. But he's well on the way. Look on to **John 19 v 39** for the moving end to the Nicodemus story.

Nicodemus points out (v 51) that they are breaking their own law! They shift their ground in v 52. They despised the "mob"; now they despise "Galilee".

To follow Jesus means losing the world's applause. Nicodemus had to be sneered at. What does it mean for you to stand openly for Jesus against the world's sneers?

Throwing the first stone

Reading: John 7 v 53 – 8 v 11 **Thursday** 17 March

Today's passage is a bit of a puzzle. It almost certainly wasn't originally part of John's Gospel. It appears in all sorts of different places in the old manuscripts (and even in Luke's Gospel sometimes!). Nevertheless, it has the ring of truth about it and seems to be a true story about Jesus. And it's a wonderful story.

Read 7 v 53 – 8 v 11

The accusation

Read v 3-6a

What was the motive of the Pharisees and co.?

Look carefully at v 6. Did they love God? Did they really care for God's honour? Did they love this sinner? And what about the man, who was presumably caught at the same time?

No, no, no! They wanted to put Jesus between a rock and a hard place. Either He was soft on the woman (in which case He would be discredited as a religious teacher) or He had to challenge the Roman law, which did not allow the Jews to lynch a person.

The challenge

Read v 6b-8

Think carefully about Jesus' challenge to them. Who has the right to act in judgment on sinful people? And who does not?

It is an amazing and deeply humbling answer.

time out

When are you tempted to sit in judgment on others, and to condemn them and want to punish them?

The trouble is, what are we to do when people do things wrong? It won't do to pretend it doesn't matter, because it does. And yet we are in no position to judge. **Read Romans 2 v 1-4.**

How ought we to respond to the sins of others?

The chance of a new life

Read v 9-11

Picture the scene as one after another slinks away, angry and ashamed of themselves. Jesus is the one person there who could throw the first stone. And yet He doesn't.

What two things does He say to the woman?

time out

What two things does Jesus say to us, if we trust in Him?

Thank and praise Him that there is no condemnation in Him. And pray that real, practical repentance ("leave your life of sin") will be ours.

The light of the world

Reading: John 8 v 12-20 **Friday** 18 March

We are still in the temple courts, as in chapter 7.

Following the light

Read v 12

What do you notice about this "light"? Is it stationary or moving?

time out

Can you think of a time in Israel's history when they had to "follow" a light? Look back at ***Exodus 13 v 21-22****.*

Jesus is the One who leads God's people into the promised land (which is a picture of the new creation). It's quite a claim: if you and I want to end up in the new heavens and new earth, we must walk behind Jesus. We'll get lost behind anyone else.

Who says so?

Read v 13-18

How many times do words like "testimony", "testify", and "witness" appear?

What's the evidence that Jesus is right?

To be sure something was true, it had to be witnessed by more than one person (see **Deuteronomy 19 v 15** for example).

What do the Pharisees accuse Jesus of?

"It's your word against ours," they say, "so how can we be sure you're telling the truth?"

What evidence does Jesus give that He is? Who is His other witness?

In v 15, "by human standards" means something like, "by appearances"—you look at the outside and fail to see who I really am. When Jesus goes on to say: "I pass judgment on no one", He probably means that—unlike the Pharisees—He came to rescue and not to condemn.

Where is your father?

Read v 19

Their question may be a snipe at the circumstances of Jesus' birth: "We've heard stories about your paternity. It sounds scandalous!"

How does Jesus answer?

God the Father is invisible. So how are people to "see" Him? Look back at ***John 1 v 18*** *as well.*

His hour had not yet come

Read v 20

Why did no one seize Jesus? After all, He was teaching in a public place. There was an "hour" (a "time") when He must die; but until that hour no one could seize Him. Who's in control? It's not His enemies!

Meditate on v 19. Praise Jesus that to know Him by faith is to know the Father God.

How not to die in our sins

Reading: John 8 v 21-30 **Saturday** 19 March

How much does it matter to believe the truth about Jesus? This passage divides into something about our deaths, and something about Jesus' death.

Our deaths

Read v 21-24

How many times does Jesus tell them they will die in their sin or sins?

Glance back at **John 7 v 33-34**; Jesus has said this before. There is nothing more serious in all eternity. To die in my sins is to die with every sin unforgiven, and therefore to endure the lonely terrors of hell, where there is no love, no beauty, no good, and no hope.

Look again at v 23

Where do we belong, by nature?

"This world" or "below" is the place of alienation from God, where people couldn't care less about God and don't honour Him. The only way to be transferred from belonging to "the world" to belonging "above" is to have God the Son as my Rescuer.

Jesus is not being unreasonable. They saw before them day after day perfect goodness lived out and wonderful miracles performed. It was all there. It was entirely their fault if they chose to reject Him.

Think about friends or family members who are not Christians. What evidence have they had? What danger are they in? How can you live and speak for Jesus to them?

Jesus' death

Read v 25-30

Jesus says He "always" does what pleases His Father.

What is the ultimate test of this obedience?

When will they know He really means this?

*What does Jesus mean by "lifted up"? Look at **John 12 v 32-33** for an explanation.*

There is a double meaning here. Crucifixion meant being literally lifted up and nailed to a cross. And yet this terrible death was also the time when Jesus' glory would be seen most clearly.

The cross proves beyond reasonable doubt that Jesus really did and does always do what pleases the Father.

It is astonishing to say: "I always do what pleases Him". Think what it meant for Jesus to do this. Pray that you will do what pleases your heavenly Father even when it is hard.

Passionate...

Reading: Psalm 116 v 1-11 **Sunday** 20 March

Fervour.
Passion for God.
Whatever happened to that?

Read Psalm 116

Do you know someone who has such a love for God that it just oozes out of them? They can't help talking about Him; can't help wanting to do the right thing for Him. This psalm's written by someone like that...

Deep, deep trouble

Read v 1-3

What is this singer so passionate about (v 1)?

What did it lead him to do (v 2)?

We're not told what crisis he faced, but it was serious (v 3, 8a). And he felt totally abandoned. In fact, the references to death suggest that it was mortal, physical danger he was facing.

But worse than that, the physical fear led to an overwhelming sense of depression and hopelessness (3b). Disaster movies show how such fear leads to different reactions in people: some give up, others look around for someone to blame and vent their anger, others scramble hopelessly for survival.

But what did the writer do (v 4)?

When trouble strikes—whether it's life-threatening, or a more run-of-the-mill snag—what is your first instinct? Do you call a friend to cry on their shoulder, go numb and stare into space, or put your head down and try and sort it out yourself? Our personalities may be predisposed to any one of these reactions, but surely the Christian response is to turn to the Lord; to cry to Him...

Read 1 Peter 5 v 6-7.

Complete and utter rescue

Read v 4-11

The rescue has a completeness and finality about it (v 8). The physical danger is removed, leading to a sense of peace (v 7), an end to anguish and a new sense of stability (v 8).

But what has the writer been saved for (v 9)?

And what else must he do (v 10)? See how ***2 Corinthians 4 v 13-15*** *interprets this.*

God's salvation always leads to two things:

- Living for and in the presence of God—walking in His ways of holiness and righteousness.
- Telling others about what He has done for us.

If these two "effects" are missing, maybe we need to ponder whether or not we have truly experienced the "cause"...

Slaves to sin

Reading: John 8 v 31-38 **Monday** 21 March

Read the whole passage

Who is Jesus speaking to (v 31)?

Why do you think He speaks so strongly against them, if they have believed in Him?

Either they *had* believed in Him in some sense in the past, but they don't any longer, or they had only "believed" in Him in a very shallow way, rather like in **John 2 v 23-25**.

Real disciples

Read v 31-32

What makes a genuine disciple?

What happens to a real disciple?

"The truth" here means the real, genuine Jesus.

Read v 33

They don't think they need setting free. Why not?

How does v 34 answer them?

Jesus is talking about being trapped in self-centred behaviour, which we cannot break free from on our own.

time out

The biggest threat to real Christianity is counterfeit religion.

What might be the modern equivalents of resting your assurance on being descended from Abraham?

What religious privileges might lead you to become complacent and assume that you will be alright?

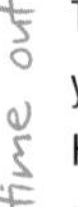

Think about particular sins from which you have tried to break free but failed. Have religious privileges helped you? You need something deeper than that!

If the Son sets you free...

Read v 35-36

Jesus uses the picture of a big household. Slaves can be dismissed at any time. But the son of the owner is always the son. If God's one and only Son sets us free to be sons and daughters of God in His family, we shall be really free. This is what we need.

time out

Jesus sets us free now from all sin's condemnation. All our sins, past, present and future, are covered by His death. He does for us what we cannot do for ourselves. By His Spirit He gradually enables us to fight sin in daily life. And one day He'll give us resurrection bodies, and we'll no longer be troubled by any temptation. Praise Him for that!

Who is your father?

Read v 36-38

They had asked Jesus where His father was (v 19). Now He raises the question of their spiritual paternity.

What evidence is there that they are not spiritually Abraham's descendants?

Paternity suit

Reading: John 8 v 39-47

Tuesday 22 March

Before DNA testing, how did you tell who someone's father was? You looked for the family likeness (the father's brown eyes etc). In the same way, we can tell what spiritual family people are in from the spiritual family likeness.

As we read today's and tomorrow's hard passages, it is important to remember Jesus is not being anti-Semitic. These verses have been used in anti-Semitic propaganda. But we must remember that Jesus Himself was a Jew and so were the apostles! No, Jesus is speaking against those who hate Him in every age. We need to ask if He needs to say these things to us!

Abraham is our father

Read v 39-41

How does Jesus prove they are not really Abraham's spiritual children?

Abraham believed God would keep His promises. If Abraham had walked on earth during Jesus' ministry, he would have been thrilled to see those promises kept!

In v 41 Jesus darkly insinuates that there is another "father" behind their behaviour. He will soon tell us who.

God is our father

Read v 41-43

They up the stakes! No longer content with Abraham, they claim God as their father! (There may be another snide dig at the circumstances of Jesus' birth when they say, "*We* are not illegitimate children".)

According to v 42, what is the family likeness that shows someone is God's spiritual child? Why?

This is very important. If anyone really belongs to God the Father, they will love Jesus. No one belongs to the Father who doesn't love Jesus.

*How would you answer someone who says they love God but doesn't see the need for being so narrow and particular in insisting on faith in **Jesus**?*

The devil's children

Read v 44-47

These are terrible verses.

Whose spiritual children are they?

How does Jesus know this?

What is this father's character? What family likeness will betray his paternity?

All hatred, murder and lies come from the devil. Whenever we turn against what we know to be good and true, we follow the devil's ways. Think about the importance of keeping absolutely true in everything you say and do.

Before Abraham, I am!

Reading: John 8 v 48-59 **Wednesday** 23 March

It matters massively who Jesus is.

Power over death

Read v 48

What two accusations do they make against Jesus?

The first is racist, and may go back to stories about Jesus' wonderful ministry in Samaria in chapter 4. The second concerns the source of His power.

Read v 49-51

Which accusation does Jesus ignore and which does He answer?

Look carefully at Jesus' answer. What does He say about His motives (v 49-50)? How do they prove He is genuine?

Then what amazing promise does He make in verse 51?

This ties back to v 12: if we follow Jesus the light into the promised land, we will be taken safely through death into the new creation.

pray thru'

It is easy to skim over verse 51. But pause and think about it. To "keep" Jesus' word means to be a faithful and persevering disciple. Pray that you will keep going as a Christian and praise Jesus for His promise about death.

Who do you think you are?

Read v 52-53

What tone of voice would they have said these things in?

Why do they think Jesus' promise is absurd?

Now think about the irony: what is the true answer to their questions?! It all comes down to *who* Jesus is.

My Father glorifies me

Read v 54-56

Why must Jesus insist on saying that He really does know and honour God?

Notice the repetition from v 51 of "keep ... word" in v 55. Jesus keeps the Father's word; and we must keep Jesus' word.

Abraham saw Christ's day

Read v 56

What do you think v 56 means?

Abraham knew what God had promised (from **Genesis 12 v 1-3** onwards through Genesis), and he believed God would keep His promise. He didn't know any details, but in principle he believed God would do all that was necessary to keep the promises.

*Look at **Hebrews 11 v 10, 13**. How does this help us understand?*

Now read v 57-59

The words "I am" here echo the sacred name of God in the Old Testament (eg: **Exodus 3 v 14**). What is Jesus claiming? It's not surprising they wanted to stone Him.

So who's blind now?

Reading: John 9 v 1-12

Thursday 24 March

"I get it." "He just doesn't get it." To "get" something is to see it clearly, to grasp it. The theme of chapter 9 is who "gets it" about Jesus.

Blind from birth

Read v 1

The last thing we read, Jesus had to slip quietly out of the temple because His enemies just didn't get it about Him (8 v 59). Now He "happens" to see a man blind from birth. It's both a fact (it happened) and a picture (it means something): Jesus *sees*; the man has never *seen*. This is us by nature. What will happen when the light of the world (8 v 12) meets a man in darkness (1 v 4-5)?

Q and A

Read v 2-3

The disciples ask what caused *this blindness. How does Jesus answer?*

There's a *purpose*. He is going to do "the work of God" in this man's life.

Read v 4-5

Why the urgency?

"Night" here seems to mean the time of the cross, when Jesus cannot make blind people see. When Judas goes out in 13 v 30 "it was night" in more senses than one.

Notice the "we" (v 4). Jesus draws in His disciples to the works of God.

A symbolic healing

Read v 6-7

Look for the word "sent" in v 7 and 4.

The water in this pool was—as it were—"sent" into Jerusalem from the Gihon spring (through the tunnel Hezekiah built—**2 Kings 20 v 20**). In the same way, sight comes to this man from the One sent by the Father, the Source of all life and light.

A faithful testimony

Read v 8-9

Who "gets it" about the ID of the man?

Only the man Jesus has made to see! The rest are scrabbling around in the dark. It's a bit like with Jesus Himself. They keep arguing about who He is; only Jesus really knows.

Read v 10-12

Compare v 11 with v 6-7.

Notice how precisely the man tells the story of his healing; And yet Jesus is still elusive (v 12). We cannot find Him; He finds us.

Think about blindness and sight. What do you find hard to grasp about Jesus?

Pray that Jesus will give you sight.

Courage and fear

Reading: John 9 v 13-23 **Friday** 25 March

In chapter 5 Jesus healed a paralysed man on the Sabbath. The man was hauled up in front of the Pharisees for carrying his bed (5 v 9-10). In chapter 9 we almost have a re-run. But with one big difference!

Divided about Jesus

Read v 13-16

They accuse Jesus of breaking the Sabbath. How?

Notice how the "mud" detail is mentioned twice. Their rules (not in the Old Testament) said you couldn't make a mud-pack on the Sabbath!

Imagine the conversations of v 16. They had a theory about the Sabbath; and they weren't going to let the evidence get in the way.

Testimony

Read v 17

It must have been an awkward moment: "What have you to say about Him?" If I had been him, I would have wanted the floor to swallow me up. But notice how his answer is stronger than before. In verse 11 he just called Jesus "the man"; now He is "a prophet". So here's the difference: this time (unlike chapter 5) the healed man gives brave testimony about Jesus.

There are times when the question comes to us, perhaps in front of unsympathetic people: "What have you to say about Jesus? You say He has opened your eyes." What do we answer? Why do we find it hard? Pray for strength to give clear, simple testimony as this man does.

Non-testimony

Read v 18-23

They ask the parents two types of question in v 19. The first is factual: "Is this your son who was born blind?" The second question shows they already know the answer to the first! "How is it that now he can see?"

Which question do the parents answer?

Why do they not answer the other one?

What were they afraid of?

time out

To be put "out of the synagogue" would hurt them socially (in terms of belonging to society) and probably economically. We see the same threat or danger in **12 v 42** and **16 v 2**.

What does it cost to bear courageous witness that Jesus is the Christ today? For you? For other believers in other parts of the world?

BIBLE IN A YEAR: **PROVERBS 6-7 • 1 CORINTHIANS 15 v 29-58**

Once I was blind; now I see

Reading: John 9 v 24-34 **Saturday** 26 March

It is one thing to resist attack. It is much harder to keep resisting sustained pressure. But that's what this baby disciple has to do. He's been brave once; but now he must be for "a second time".

Witness for the prosecution?

Read v 24

The man's parents had passed the buck (v 23); they don't want to take any risks, and they'd rather he got into trouble—the cowards. "Give glory to God" is an expression that means: "Promise to tell the truth"; the Pharisees swear the man in to give legal testimony.

What do they claim to "know"? Why?

Look back at v 16. They want the man to say something that will incriminate Jesus further. He is sworn in as witness for the prosecution. But he will speak courageously for the defence!

One thing I know

Read v 25-27

What does the man "know"? He sticks with what he's certain about. When they pester him, not satisfied with his simple true answers, he teases them: "Do you want to become his disciples, too?" Clearly he counts himself as a disciple now. He knows they don't. It's very brave.

Evidence that demands a verdict

Read v 28-29

How do they speak negatively of Jesus?

What do they call Him?

He has a name (v 11), but they don't use it. What do they hold against Him? Back in 7 v 27 they say they do know where He came from! They are not very consistent.

Read v 30-34

Look at the logic of the man's answer in v 30-33. They can't answer his logic. Notice how v 34 is not argument, but insult. It's a case of "argument weak, shout louder".

time out

Their response to clear evidence reveals their rebellious hearts. How do we see the same today when the evidence for Jesus is presented to people?

How does the passage end (v 34)?

That's just what his parents had feared (v 22).

pray thru'

All this time, the man hasn't even seen Jesus! Think about his courage and pray to be like him, to stand up clearly for Jesus in front of other people.

Sight reversals

Reading: John 9 v 35-41 **Sunday** 27 March

The man born blind has been thrown out of Jewish society (v 34). And now something wonderful happens to him. Someone has said the man was: "cast out of the temple, and the Lord of the temple found him ... Such are the prizes of truth."

Faith seeking understanding

Read v 35

The man is thrown out.

- *What happens next? Who finds whom?*
- *Does the man search for his Healer, or does his Healer search for him?*

Read v 36-38

- *How does v 36 give us a window into the man's heart?*

He doesn't have much understanding yet and he doesn't know very much. But he knows he can see, he knows Jesus healed him, and he wants to believe. What a contrast to the Pharisees!

- *How can you tell the difference between someone who doesn't understand but wants to believe, and someone who will not understand because they choose not to believe?*

What a wonderful answer Jesus gives (v 37) and what a marvellous response from the man (v 38)!

- *How does v 37 complete the man's "sight"?*

He is given eyes in order that he may see the Son of Man; that's what his eyes are for. The whole story is a picture of being given spiritual sight.

Jesus' two-edged ministry

Now read v 39

This seems to be a general public announcement to anyone who is listening.

- *What two things happened when Jesus walked on earth?*
- *How has our story shown us both of them?*

Read v 40-41

Jesus' statement worries the Pharisees (v 40).

- *Think carefully about Jesus' answer (v 41). What makes the Pharisees so guilty?*

It's not a lack of understanding. After all, the blind man started with no sight at all and only gradually got it about Jesus. No, it's being so sure they know it all, when actually they don't get it at all.

time out

Think about how gradually real understanding about Jesus can come. Look at how the healed man calls Jesus "the man" in v 11, "a prophet" in v 17, someone sent "from God" in v 33, and finally worships Him in v 38.

- *What is your experience so far of understanding the things of Jesus?*
- *How does this give you hope?*

Life to the full

Reading: John 10 v 1-10 **Monday** 28 March

One of the greatest plagues on the Christian church down the ages has been church leaders who are not even Christians! It was the same in Jesus' day. In fact the most hostile people were the most religious people.

The shepherd's voice

*Who is Jesus talking to? Look back to **9 v 40**.*

*What had these people just done to the man born blind? Look back to **9 v 34**.*

Read v 1-5

Don't get bogged down in the details. It's a simple middle-eastern picture. A sheep fold keeps sheep from several flocks safe overnight. In the morning the shepherds come in and call their own sheep out.

How do the sheep know their particular shepherd? Look for the same word in each of verses 3, 4, and 5. It's very emphatic!

In chapter 9, when the man gave his brave testimony to Jesus, all he knew of Jesus was His voice. He didn't actually *see* Jesus until afterwards (9 v 37).

Now read v 6 and look for the irony

These Pharisees who were listening—did they recognise the Shepherd's voice?!

Have there been times for you when you have known someone wasn't teaching the truth, even if you couldn't really explain exactly why not?

I remember as a very young Christian that happening to me. I would listen to a preacher and it just sounded *wrong*. This is the sheep running away from a stranger's voice.

The shepherd's gate

Read v 7-9

The picture changes slightly. If you're going to be a proper shepherd (a leader of Jesus' people), you need to come "through" Jesus yourself first and become one of His sheep.

Had the Pharisees done this? Why not?

The shepherd's purpose

Read v 10

What is the false "Christian" leader in it for?

And what is the true Shepherd's aim?

time out

Read Ezekiel 34, where you'll see a terrible picture of the bad leaders of God's people.

How can this happen today? Think of ways in which people become church leaders because of what's in it for them.

The good Shepherd

Reading: John 10 v 11-21 **Tuesday** 29 March

How is the Good Shepherd going to give "life to the full" to His sheep (v 10)? ***Read the passage.***

A. The cross is essential

Read v 11

How often in the rest of the passage does Jesus talk about "laying down His life" for the sheep?

This is what makes Jesus different. We cannot have "life to the full" unless our Shepherd lays down His life in our place.

Jesus now teaches three more wonderful truths about the cross.

B. The cross proves how much He cares

Read v 12-15

Why isn't a "hired" farm labourer willing to make a personal sacrifice to protect the sheep?

What motivates him is his wages, not his love.

By contrast, how well does Jesus know and love His sheep? Look at the amazing comparison He gives in v 15.

C. The cross has the whole world in view

Read v 16

The "sheep pen" of the Jewish people contains some who are really Jesus' sheep and some who are not (such as most of the Pharisees). But what about the rest of the world, in the Gentile "sheep pen"? All over the world there are men and women who are Jesus' sheep and need to be called and brought in.

What will they do when He brings them?

Notice the same theme of His *voice* we saw in verses 3, 4, and 5 yesterday.

What is the final result?

time out

At the moment the human race is as scattered and broken as at the Tower of Babel (**Genesis 11 v 1-9**). One day Christ will head one redeemed humanity together under His leadership. **Read Ezekiel 34 v 23-24**, and notice how both God (the Father) and Christ (the King in David's line) are involved.

D. The cross was planned by the Father's love

Read v 17-18

What has the Father commanded and given Jesus power to do?

This is what the Father's love means; He loves Jesus because Jesus perfectly shares His love and does what His love wants.

Read v 19-21

They don't understand at all.

Thank Jesus for being the true Leader and for all that His death means for us.

As safe as safe can be

Reading: John 10 v 22-30 **Wednesday** 30 March

Three great questions are set before us today.

Is Jesus the Christ?

Read v 22-24

The Feast of Tabernacles (chapter 7) was in October. Now it's December, and Jesus is again in Jerusalem.

? *What was the really big question people were asking?*

Notice the word "plainly". When a pupil in school asks a teacher to make something clearer, it means one of two things: either the teacher isn't very good, or the pupils are very dim! Maybe it will never be clear enough for them. Which is it here?!

Why don't they believe?

Read v 25

? *Jesus says He **has** made the answer plain. How?*

Now read v 26

? *What reason does Jesus give for their not believing?*

It wasn't His bad teaching, or second-rate miracles! Jesus could teach forever and do millions more amazing miracles, and still they would not believe.

time out

If some people are "Jesus' sheep" and some are not, what is the point of telling people the gospel? Actually, it's the opposite: because some people are Jesus' sheep (and we don't know who they are), it is worth calling people to faith in Jesus, knowing that some people will respond. So it's an encouragement to evangelism!

How safe are you if you do believe?

Now read v 27-28

? *What two things does v 27 tell us that Jesus' sheep do?*

? *And what one thing about Jesus?*

? *What is the promise of v 28?*

Jesus puts it positively and negatively. Notice that a sheep is in Jesus' "hand". But how strong is Jesus' "hand"? **Read v 29-30 to see.**

? *How did the sheep get into Jesus' hand? Who put them there?*

? *And who therefore guards them with Jesus?*

There is, as it were, a double-divine guard over us if we are real Christians.

When do you feel that your Christian faith is fragile and you may be swept out of Jesus' hand by forces outside your control? Think about sudden tragedies, or the lure of the world, or the deception of plausible but false "Christian" teachers. Thank Jesus and the Father for their strong hand of safety on your life.

Some people never learn

Reading: John 10 v 31-42 **Thursday** 31 March

What would you do if you saw in front of your eyes a life lived with perfect goodness and showing perfect loving power? It's easy to give the answer we'd like to give; but what would we actually do? For some people 2000 years ago that was exactly the question they faced.

Religious anger

Read v 31-33

Why are they so angry?

Look back to **v 28-30**. What did Jesus mean there by saying that He and the Father were "one"? Look what the Son and the Father do with their "hand". They do the same. They keep safe exactly the same people. They act to rescue in perfect harmony. All the Father does to rescue people, the Son does.

An Old Testament answer

Read v 34-36

Jesus quotes from a psalm to show that the Old Testament can even call human beings "gods". So what's so outrageous about calling *this unique human being* "the Son of God"?!

time out

Read Psalm 82. The "gods" here would seem to be the "assembly" of Israel. It was a wonderful privilege to be an Old Testament Israelite. Even though they sinned and died, they could be called "gods". How much more appropriate is it to call Jesus, who never sinned, "God".

Believing miracles

What evidence did they have?

Look carefully through v 32 and then v 37-38

Even if they are not prepared to listen to what Jesus has to *say* for Himself, He wants them at least to look at what He *does*. The "miracles" are evidence that Jesus does exactly what the Father does. He could not do them if not.

Believing testimony

Now look at the contrast in v 39-42

Jesus' opponents won't even believe amazing miracles, because they are not Jesus' sheep. Now Jesus slips away to the area where John the Baptist had baptised. Look at what they say. No need for miracles here. They believe what John had said about Jesus.

apply

Think about miracles and testimony.

Which is more impressive to the world?

But which brings deep and lasting faith? Why?

Pray that you will be a faithful witness, bearing honest testimony to Jesus.

gospel-centred
Life
becoming the person God want you to be
Relationships
Decisions
Suffering
Gospel
Friends
Possessions
Horizons
2009
gospel-centred
Life
becoming the person God wants you to be
Steve Timmis Tim Chester
How can ordinary Christians live the truly extraordinary life that God calls us to? In this exciting new study guide Steve Timmis and Tim Chester help us to see that it is only possible by keeping the gospel at the heart of everything we do. Ideal to use individually, in a Bible study or in a prayer group.

Details over the page...

Time with God

your introduction to a regular time with God

This short guide is designed to help you make time with God a part of your daily routine. With daily readings, prompts and advice, it will encourage you to seek out a consistent time and place where you can nurture and grow your relationship with God, and discover the joy and liberty that come from knowing Him. It includes 28 daily Bible readings and articles, advice, and practical tips on how to apply what the passage teaches. Get hold of a copy of *Time with God* for yourself, or anyone else you know who struggles to make time with God a regular thing.

UK: www.thegoodbook.co.uk
N America: www.thegoodbook.com
Australia: www.thegoodbook.com.au
N Zealand: www.thegoodbook.co.nz

In the next issue

- John
- 1 Chronicles
- 2 Chronicles
- Easter
- Psalms

Don't miss your copy. Contact your local Christian bookshop or church agent, or go to one of the websites listed below, to get the next issue.

Contact us...

UK & EUROPE
www.thegoodbook.co.uk
t: 0333 123 0880
e: admin@thegoodbook.co.uk

AUSTRALIA
www.thegoodbook.com.au
t: (02) 6100 4211
e: admin@www.thegoodbook.com.au

N AMERICA
www.thegoodbook.com
t (toll free): 866 244 2165
e: sales@thegoodbook.com

NEW ZEALAND
www.thegoodbook.co.nz
t: (+64) 3 343 1990

SOUTH AFRICA
www.christianbooks.co.za
t: (021) 674 6931/2

Introduce a friend to Explore!

If you're enjoying using *Explore*, why not introduce a friend? Visit your local website to order our introductory issue: *Time with God*.

Contributors

Christopher Ash (John) is the director of the Cornhill Training Course in London.

Tim Chester (1 Chronicles) is part of the Crowded House network in Sheffield, UK.

Tim Thornborough (Philippians, Psalms) works at The Good Book Company.

Anne Woodcock (Genesis) works at The Good Book Company. Special thanks to **John Richardson** (a minister in Elsenham and Ugley in Essex, UK) for his source material on Genesis.

Editor: Tim Thornborough.

Production team: Alison Mitchell, Nicole Carter, Anne Woodcock.

Cover design: André Parker.